The forests were fu
hung in innumerable clust
more precipitous hillsides,
grew. Sweet and clean, the September air blew through miles
upon miles of ripening fruits and nuts. Looking south Henry
Hudson saw stretching away that wonderful sheet of water that
has been called the most beautiful bay in the world; and to the
north his eye ranged the vista beyond the unique bosses of the
Palisades.

Somewhere between the ragged heights of Weehawken and the
commanding slope of Fort Washington, on the morning of the
thirteenth of September, 1609, Henry Hudson stood on
the deck of the Half Moon and knew that though the fates had
warred against him—he had not failed.

–from *Henry Hudson: His Times and His Voyages*

HENRY HUDSON HIS TIMES AND HIS VOYAGES

BY

EDGAR MAYHEW BACON

PRESS
HVA Press
Warwick, NY

Published by HVA Press

This edition copyright © 2019 by HVA Press, LLC

Henry Hudson: His Times and His Voyages was first published in 1907.

This book was scanned from an early edition of the original work. The interior scan of this book is the property of HVA Press, LLC. All rights reserved.

The HVA logo and "The History of New York is the History of America" are trademarks of HVA Press, LLC.

Cover design by Daniel Rembert

Print ISBN: 978-1-948697-06-4

Manufactured in the United States of America

HVA Press
Warwick, NY
HVAPress.com

PREFACE

N offering a monograph upon the times and voyages of Henry Hudson, the author cannot hope to add to the student's store of knowledge much that is unfamiliar in detail, but he believes that by a new collection and arrangement of data a novel and important presentation of the navigator may be submitted.

Hudson was a man of energy, a fact abundantly proved by the testimony of his contemporaries, as well as by the several records attributed to himself and his subordinates; that he may be classed as an American man of energy depends upon the elasticity of a word. To be an American at this day implies that one has been to the manner born, or that he has acquired citizenship by residence for a term of years; a century and a quarter ago Lafayette became a citizen by special act of Congress; three hundred years ago Henry Hudson became an American by virtue of his American explorations, other requirements not having been formulated. For the purposes of this work he may be accepted without cavil as an American Man of Energy.

Preface

In this book the attention of the reader will be called particularly to the great forces that at the beginning of the seventeenth century were re-forming history, and that were impelling men of character to occupy new fields of endeavour and discovery. In all classes of society, there was the leaven of a great unrest, and the minds of men were attentive as never before to the call of ambition and the allurements of conquest.

Henry Hudson was the normal product of a great epoch. Neither before nor since his time could any man have conceived a project at once so reasonable and so unreasonable, so dependent upon sober logic and upon baseless fable, upon newly awakened knowledge and old superstition, as that which urged him to strive again and again to penetrate the barriers of an unknown West for a pathway to an impossible East.

It was the consequence of the times in which he lived that every known effort of Hudson's life was baffled or at least hampered by the men who sailed with him. In this book I shall try to make clear that the signal achievement upon which rests his principal claim to immortality was largely the result of accident, but accident so controlled by qualities akin to genius that the very elements of failure became the foundations of his success.

It will be shown in the pages which follow that Hudson was turned aside by an ungovernable crew from the prosecution of the plan to which in 1609 he was pledged, and that he seemed for a time to be destined to become the sport of chance ; but by the exercise of a fraction of his rightful authority, by the use of such diplomatic skill as he possessed, and by the buoyancy of an unyielding hope, he accomplished a feat that would have been creditable to an explorer who rode upon the very crest of the wave of fortune, and forever established his right to be included among the world's men of energy.

In the unfolding of this story, we shall see that the voyage which made Hudson famous was hastened by an intrigue, partly political, in which the King of France had a share. It will also be noticed that at the conclusion of that voyage and for several succeeding years the Hollanders, in whose service Hudson sailed, showed no appreciation of the value of his explorations, and that neither the makers of their charts nor the governing boards of their merchants deemed his achievements on the American coast worth mention till some time after his death.

Hudson was not a Hollander by birth, residence, language, nor sympathy. To give to his name a Dutch equivalent, and to picture him as one expatriated from his own land is wide of historic fact, and may be reckoned on a par with the feat of Michael Angelo in putting horns upon his Moses. It is probable that the inability of the English navigator to use the language of the Dutch portion of his crew was one of the causes of their mutiny, and if this view is correct it adds to the glory of his subsequent success.

As far as the life of Hudson is known, it is contained in the records of four voyages, undertaken in four successive years, years which were crowded with adventure and achievement. The fragmentary journals from which the historian must piece together the narrative of the navigator's wanderings give sufficient indication of a brave, resourceful, manly spirit. Hudson was not by any means devoid of the faults that were common to mariners and landsmen in his day, but he exhibited more than an average share of their virtues. The principal sources from which the immediate narrative of Hudson's explorations is drawn may be briefly enumerated. Most of them are filtered through the pages of the Reverend Samuel Purchas, in which transmission much has been lost. For the first voyage, accomplished in 1607, we have an account that was written partly by one John Playse or Pleyce, a member of his crew. Pleyce's journal was evidently intended for his own use, not for publication, and is therefore the more valuable. There is little to add to his simple commentary, that interests the lay reader in spite of its professional brevity and lack of literary style.

The second voyage, in 1608, is recorded in *Purchas his Pilgrimage* with the following caption:

" A second voyage or employment of Master Henry Hudson, for finding a passage to the East Indies by the North East; *written by himselfe*."

In a footnote Purchas adds, "I have Robert Juet's journal also, for brevity omitted." This Robert Juet was Hudson's mate upon the second or 1608 voyage.

It is a matter for deep regret that his account should have been suffered to be lost.

Of the third voyage, that of 1609, undertaken for the Dutch merchants, more has been written than of all the other adventures of Hudson combined, yet in sifting our evidence we find but few trustworthy authorities. Juet, clerk and possibly second mate, has given us the major part of the data from which we must construct the story of that voyage. Hudson's own account is fragmentary and generally transmitted at second hand. Van Meterin, who wrote in Dutch, got his information at first hand and serves as a corrective to the partisan Juet. John de Laet's version of Hudson's adventures is open to criticism as being a biassed statement, by a member of the Dutch West India Company, written principally with the object of proving the validity of the Dutch claims to the province of New Netherland. The same cloud rests upon the accounts given by Adrian Van der Donck and Lambrechtsen Van Rittheim, who both wrote with a brief. The English having claimed the lands that the Dutch possessed, the assumption of title by the latter was re-inforced by such publications as Van der Donck's *Nieuw Nederlandt*, and Lambrechtsen's history.

President Jeannin, French envoy to the Netherlands, wrote a letter to Henry IV. in which light is thrown upon Hudson's negotiations in Amsterdam; the archives at The Hague furnish some material of a similar character; and the collections of the New York Historical Society supply many useful hints, though little of an important nature. The researches of John Romeyn Brodhead and others are mainly valuable because of the side-lights they throw upon the main narrative of Hudson's exploits.

For the last voyage, that of 1610, we have several documents, the most important being *An Abstract from Henry Hudson's Journal*, a *Larger Discourse on the Same Voyage*, by Abacuk Prickett, the *Detectio Freti* of Hessel Gerritz, and memoranda of Wyndhouse and others. Altogether the data are meagre and not entirely satisfactory. There are few men so well known as Hudson of whom so little is known.

For a great many years, the reports of certain Dutch writers, whose histories and memorials can be regarded as by no means unbiassed, were taken as the basis for all popular treatises substantiating Dutch claims to New Netherland lands and waters. A general summary of the statements so long relied upon as authentic may be found in the opening paragraph of a remonstrance directed to the Lords States General of Holland, by certain deputies from New Netherland, in the year 1646.

> Among all the enterprising people in the world who searched for foreign countries, navigable waters, and trade, those who bear the name of Netherlanders will very easily be able to hold their rank among the foremost, as is sufficiently known to all who have in any wise saluted the threshold of history. It will in like manner be also confirmed by our following relation, for in the year of Christ 1609 was the country of which we now

purpose to speak founded and discovered at the
expense of the West India Company (though
directing their aim and design elsewhere), by the
ship *Halve Mane*, whereof Henry Hudson was
master and factor. It was afterwards named New
Netherland by our people, and that very justly,
for it was first discovered and taken possession of
by Netherlanders and at their expense; so that
even at the present date (1646) the natives of the
country (who are so old as to remember the event)
testify that on seeing the Dutch ships on their
first coming here, they knew not what to make of
them and could not comprehend whether they
came down from Heaven or whether they were
devils. Some among them on its first approach
even imagined it to be a fish or some sea monster,
so that a strange rumour concerning it flew
throughout the whole country. We have heard
the Indians also frequently say that they knew
of no other world or people previous to the arrival
of the Netherlanders here.

The most glaring of several errors contained in the
foregoing extract is that claiming the discovery of
New Netherland for the West India Company, which,
as I have elsewhere pointed out, was not organised till
five years after Hudson's great voyage.

The reader's attention will be particularly called to
the claims of the pre-Hudsonian discoverers who may
have carried the flags of France or Spain as far as
Manhattan Island or beyond.

Perhaps the most curious of the many attempts to
prove that the *Half Moon* was not the first European

vessel to pass Manhattan Island and the Palisades is that which would make Henry Hudson his own rival. During the controversy between that renowned governor of New Netherland, Peter Stuyvesant, and some of his English neighbours who were seeking to encroach upon the Dutch territory, the statement was gravely made that several years previous to the voyage of the *Half Moon*, Henry Hudson, while in the employ of the English, had discovered and explored the North River. It must be admitted that this claim was never substantiated.

CONTENTS

xi

HENRY HUDSON

HENRY HUDSON

CHAPTER I

INTRODUCTORY

O understand a man's motives, to measure his work, or to form a just estimate of his character, it is necessary to know something of the age in which he lived and the influences and conditions that directed or modified his thought. To study Henry Hudson's life and voyages we are obliged to investigate as carefully as possible his environment. In the following pages particular attention will be invited to the closely allied mercantile and maritime enterprises of the sixteenth century, with some references to the causes and effects of the great energy that inspired them, and a brief glance at some of the men who conducted them. First, however, we shall sketch in outline the central character of our history.

An older Henry Hudson, supposed to have been the grandfather of the navigator, was an alderman in the city of London. His arms are described as "argent,

semée of fleurs-de-lis gules, a cross engrailed sable.''
His tomb in the old parish church of St. Dunstan's in
the East bears this inscription :

> Here lyeth Henry Heardson's corps,
> Within this Tombe of Stone :
> His soul (through faith in Christ's death,)
> To God in Heaven is gone.
> Whiles that he lived an Alderman
> And skinner was his state :
> To Vertue bare hee all his love,
> To Vice bare he his hate.
> He had to wife one Barbara
> Which made this tombe you see
> By whom he had of issue store,
> Eight sonnes and daughters three.
> Obiit 22. Decemb. An. Dom. 1555.

This ancestor of our navigator was one of those who
shared with Sebastian Cabot in the establishment of
the Muscovy Company, of which we shall have more
to say hereafter. There is every reason to believe that
Henry Hudson's training was gained in the service
of that company, and he was influenced by the traditions of the house he served to look in the direction
pointed out by Cabot, and after him by Davis and
Frobisher, for a short route through polar seas to the
semi-fabulous empire of Cathay.

We are not warranted, by the evidence at hand, in
attributing to Hudson any novel theories nor many
startling original discoveries, but we are justified in
thinking him an intrepid, skilful, persevering explorer,

a man of more than ordinary fineness and strength of character. He was certainly a contributor to the world's store of knowledge, and a promotor of enterprises that have added to its progress, and is therefore entitled to our serious consideration.

It detracts nothing from our estimate of this remarkable man to acknowledge the explorations and labours of others who preceded him. The chief value of his third and greatest voyage was not in its novelty, but in its thoroughness and timeliness. We believe that previous to 1609 geographers had some information concerning a stream that flowed southward and debouched into the ocean about the latitude and longitude of Manhattan Island. There is hardly room for a doubt on this subject. There is, however, a possibility that the student of history may overestimate the importance of vague and unsatisfactory maps and journals touching upon certain coasts or rivers.

We shall presently examine the claims of the pre-Hudsonian voyagers, among them Verazzano and Gomez, who probably accomplished the passage of the Narrows before Hudson was born. Verazzano's account was long disputed, though now generally accepted ; Gomez and others have received tardy and reluctant credence. We are led to suppose that one went up the river as far as the north end of Manhattan Island and that another possibly proceeded as far as Poughkeepsie ; one cartographer engraved a Rio Grande hereabout and another located a river which he called Saint Anthony in the same latitude. Looking away from these somewhat misty records to the clearer account of Hudson's voyages we do not find in the latter any vagueness nor room for doubt. The story of his adventures, though fragmentary, is in all essential particulars clear and unequivocal. We may consent to abandon Hudson the discoverer, but we insist upon doing honour to Hudson the explorer. The merchant, the colonist, and posterity are justified in making him the titular hero of the river that has been named in his honour.

His work had the somewhat rare merit of being thorough. There has probably been no accredited discoverer in any field of art or science who has not been found to be a follower in the footsteps of some earlier discoverer. The forerunners of Henry Hudson achieved little that was of importance to mankind, while his exploration of the river that bears his name has justly placed him among the immortals.

There have been almost as many estimates of the character of Henry Hudson as there have been writers who have tried to present his life and voyages from a novel point of view. These estimates range from unreasoning adulation to unreasonable censure ; they run a gamut from the pleasant things that good nature dictates to the bitter attacks of scribes to whom all accepted theories are anathema.

Forty years ago a reverend writer who published a dissertation on the discovery of the Hudson River described Henry Hudson as "a man of fair courage and persevering, but not original or great in any sense of the terms; his, we are informed, was a respectable mediocrity; in navigation he had no new conceptions, but was rather a copyist. *This being so, we might infer at the outset* that he was not the first to discover the river that bears his name." Had Dr. De Costa been a logician, he would not have uttered so flagrant a *non sequitur*. His argument was that because he thought Henry Hudson was not original, and because he considered him a mere copyist, therefore Hudson did not discover anything. Dr. De Costa went still further in his effort to damn Hudson with faint praise. "The character of Hudson," he says, "judged by the age in which he lived, was tolerably fair; though of course hardly superior to ordinary examples."

As the exponent of a sound, sane, conservative opinion, stands the scholarly Dr. E. B. O'Callaghan, who refers to Hudson as "an intrepid English mariner, whose name has been immortalised by his valuable discoveries," though for "discoveries" in this connection we should write "explorations." Henry R. Cleveland's estimate of Hudson, included in Sparks's Biographies, and quoted elsewhere in this book, voices the sentiment of the more extreme enthusiasts who occupy a position as far removed as possible from that of the Reverend Dr. De Costa. We may form our own opinion upon certain definite facts, supplemented by reports that are generally conceded to be fairly accurate. Among the latter are the journals of Pleyce and Juet and the account of the last voyage as given by Prickett, whose story must be taken with a grain of salt whenever his narrative may be supposed to have been intended to serve personal ends. The least favourable account we have of Hudson's character is that of this man, who consented by silence and inaction to the murder of his chief, and who could most effectually insure safety for himself by aspersing the deeds and motives of one whom in his cowardice he deserted.

The charges that have been preferred against Hudson may be briefly stated. Upon his first voyage he sailed in a direction quite different from that proposed either by himself or his employers. He made a futile attempt to explore coasts already discovered, and spent all the summer of 1607 in running back and forth along a shore where nothing seemed certain but variable winds. Almost daily he changed his course, always presenting what appears a valid excuse for doing so. He pushed forward towards Greenland for a second time, apparently fascinated by the idea that Davis Straits would prove to be the long-hoped-for gateway to the eastern ocean, but gave up this quest after a few days of trial and turned the prow of the *Hopewell* towards home. In answer to the criticisms implied in these admissions, we can but point out that Hudson used all means at his command to escape a barrier of ice which was actually insurmountable and that he tried at every point to find a passage that did not exist. His failure cannot, therefore, be reasonably set down to his discredit. On the contrary it should be noticed that he penetrated further to the northward than any

Englishman of his time, that he made observations that have a distinct scientific value, and that the men of his own generation, navigators and geographers of no mean repute, considered his exploits remarkable.

On his second voyage he was driven back by invincible polar ice while attempting to find the passage in a northeasterly direction, and spent most of his time, until his provisions were exhausted, exploring an inlet in Nova Zembla. Again it is to be said that the conditions and not the navigator were to blame for the failure.

Hudson's third and most important voyage was mainly prosecuted in disobedience to sailing orders, and led him into regions that his employers had never contemplated exploring. Had it not been for the mutiny of his crew it would never have been celebrated. The fourth voyage was, like the others, essentially unsuccessful, if success must be restricted to the carrying out to the letter plans formed in advance, and it ended in the death of the explorer and his companions; but it must not be forgotten that the main narrative of this tragic expedition was written by one whose veracity may well be questioned.

That Hudson permitted his men to assault peaceful Indians is a charge that will be discussed elsewhere; that he allowed several Indians to become intoxicated while on board the *Half Moon* is stated by Juet and is probably true. The accounts of his petulance, unfair dealing towards his men, and obstinacy while on the Hudson Bay voyage, are charges mainly to be found in the narrative of the cowardly Prickett, and are probably untrue.

In an account of Hudson's third and fourth voyages, written in Latin and published in 1612 by Hessel Gerritz, a Hollander, there is a very remarkable statement and a no less astonishing admission regarding his expedition in 1609, while he was in the service of the Dutch East India Company. The passage to which I refer has been translated as follows: "He did set out, but achieved nothing to the east; he sailed therefore straight westward to attempt again the way searched out and drawn by Captain Windwood, which way after passing for about a hundred leagues through a narrow channel leads out into a wide sea. Hudson hoped to find a way through this sea, though Plantius had proved to him the impossibility of success from the accounts of a man who had reached the western shore of that sea. *Hudson achieved in 1609 nothing memorable even by this new way.*" The significance of this passage lies in the fact that in 1612 the exploration of the great North River of New Netherland was not thought worthy even a passing mention by a Dutch geographer.

Few of the navigators who preceded Hudson or who were his contemporaries paid the charges of their own voyages. In one or two instances only are we told that some master mariner like Cabot or Beverin fitted out an expedition at his own expense, and even in these cases there is room for question. The sovereigns of England, France, Spain, and Portugal, as well as the electors and princes of the Netherlands, became in turn the patrons of navigators and explorers, but these great personages were not by any means the sole, nor even the chief promoters of maritime enterprise. Back of royalty stood the merchants and nobles who measured their crowns and ducats against the glittering chance of new markets and new possessions. Frequently the merchants alone undertook to despatch vessels under the charge of experienced navigators to open new avenues for competition with traders of other lands. Great companies were organised in all the leading maritime cities of the world, particularly when the political relations between Spain and Holland were severed and the merchants of the latter country were debarred from some of the markets they had previously enjoyed. Turning their attention to the establishment of new avenues for trade the merchants of the Netherlands were thrown into close competition with England, where every one, from the throne to the shipyards, seemed imbued with a spirit of discovery, adventure, and gain.

The great companies that before Hudson's day were formed for the purpose of controlling the trade of the world, and particularly of finding some new way to the treasures of India and China, form a background for all that the historian may record in these pages.

The period included between the end of the fifteenth century and the middle of the seventeenth was one of the most remarkable recorded in history. It was an epoch during which an infectious passion for maritime adventure led to a rapid extension of geographical knowledge, and ultimately to a radical change in the economic conditions governing Christendom. A similar impulse at widely separated periods extended the dominion of Tyre and Venice, but the new movement was as imcomparably greater than any preceding one as Europe was greater than any of the states of the Mediterranean.

The age of so-called chivalry and romance, the long nightmare of feudal misgovernment, was past. While social equality, or even an approach to such a relation between high-born and low-born, seemed as remote as the promised millenium, yet already in several cities of Northern Europe were opened the doors which in the end should lead to political liberty, and in the market and exchange the future of democracy was assured. In the time of Elizabeth and Maurice of Orange burghers and commoners became merchant princes, with whom nobles and kings entered into partnership, not only lending their names to commercial ventures, but themselves instigating and controlling operations that were imperial in their magnitude. The Muscovy Company of England fostered, by every means known to merchants and mariners, the spirit of adventure, the thirst for discovery that the explorations of Cabot, Frobisher, and Davis had fathered. The men who were trained in the service of that company were filled with a zeal for maritime achievement that was only second to the enthusiasm that animated the followers of Peter the Hermit in their crusade to reconquer the Holy Sepulchre.

Since merchants first sent ships so sea, and bartered for products of foreign lands, they have formed associations for mutual protection and advantage. Even in mediæval times such companies existed and not infrequently wielded sovereign power. Out of many small companies and local organisations several larger ones were formed during the sixteenth century, and as they operated upon an increasingly extensive scale, under royal charters and articles of incorporation that gave them supreme influence, they finally monopolised the greater part of the commerce of the known world.

Historians formerly were prone to treat the story of nations as though they were setting forth the biographies of kings, eliminating the really important factors without which the narrative of kings would become but a pitiful tale of paupers. The saner, truer, modern method is to dwell not so much upon the glory of great personages as the course of great influences. We have recently begun to recognise in the development of history the potency of the merchant, the man of the bourse and the market. Europe's progress, like that of America, has depended upon the great merchants and associations of merchants who have financed all of its memorable enterprises.

Among the earliest and most powerful of the mercantile organisations of the Old World was the company known as the Merchants Adventurers of England. The date of its incorporation has not been ascertained, but was probably not later than the thirteenth century. The home of the association was in London, and its members were generally mercers, or, as we would say, dry-goods merchants. Any one might share the advantages of the mercers' guild by paying a "fine" or entrance fee. The control of the very lucrative cloth trade between England and the Low Countries was largely in the hands of the Merchants Adventurers, who were so protected that they were able to impose prohibitive tolls upon all imports that did not pass through their hands. In the fourteenth century this great corporation procured special privileges from the Count of Flanders and made a profit in the rich products of the Flemish looms. Other concessions from other powers followed, till the Merchants Adventurers were known in all lands and sent their ships to all seas, while at home their influence was enormous.

When that monster of cruelty and oppression, Ivan the Terrible, to whom Elizabethan writers refer as "Ivan Vasilivitch, Duke of Muscovy," was occupying the throne that has descended to the Czars of Russia, some English merchants succeeded in establishing trade with Muscovy through the port of Archangel: furthermore they obtained from Ivan special concessions that were favourable to English commerce. The first of the Czars was at that time greatly in need of a powerful ally who should take part with him in thwarting the schemes of the obnoxious Hansa on the one hand, and keep in check the neighbouring powers of Poland and Sweden on the other. England was just that friend for whom Ivan wished, and his overtures to Elizabeth commenced with a proposal for a defensive alliance and ended more than a decade afterwards with an offer of his hand to the Queen's niece, Maria Hastings, Countess of Huntingdon. The history of these negotiations is one of keen interest to the historian. The passionate outbursts of the Czar against Elizabeth's ministers, who are characterised in one of his letters to her as "people who rule independent of you, who neither regard our sovereign presence nor think of the honour nor dignity of our state," led to open ruptures, succeeded by new overtures as the pressure of the Terrible's jealous neighbours became unbearable.

At no time did the Queen or her advisers regard the proposed alliance with favour, yet whenever they offended the Muscovite ruler a cry went up from the merchants, who had succeeded in establishing an intermittent trade with Russia by means of the port of Archangel. Ivan Vasilivitch when enraged retaliated upon the ministers by restricting the operations of the merchants, withdrawing privileges granted when anticipating success. When the Czar was pleased the Englishmen were allowed to pursue a lucrative traffic with Persia, to search for ore in the province of Archangel, and enjoy a monopoly of the trade of the White Sea. The English commercial headquarters or factory in Russia was placed under the special protection of the Opritchniks, the savage body-guard of the no less savage ruler.

When Elizabeth's somewhat left-handed essays in diplomacy angered the Terrible, he revoked all the favours he had granted to the merchants, and, not content with that, he confiscated their goods. Nevertheless through the reign of Ivan and his successors the Russia or Muscovy Company gradually succeeded in the aims for which it had been organised.

Speaking of the service rendered by the Muscovy Company to navigators and geographers, Dr. Georg M. Asher makes the following remarkable statement: "The *log-book*, the most admirable of all the inventions for the furtherance of that science [navigation] owed its origin and development to the Muscovy Company. How greatly navigation and geography are indebted to them for this service appears chiefly when we compare Verazzano's account of his voyage to Hudson's river with Juet's journal of Hudson's expedition to the same coasts. We observe Verazzano, a man of great talent, making painful efforts to convey a clear meaning, and succeeding but indifferently, whilst Juet, a man of ordinary abilities, furnishes us with an account in which every step can be clearly traced. Nor is Verazzano's failure or Juet's success at all isolated. Verazzano's narrative is very nearly the best maritime record of his period, whilst Juet's journal is in every respect surpassed by many anterior log-books. The difference between Juet and Verazzano, as far as it is to the disadvantage of the latter, consists not in their respective talents, but in the methods they made use of."

When the Portuguese merchants began to bring oriental fabrics and many curious wares from the East to the Flemish market, the English traders lost little time in introducing these delectable goods to a court that had already acquired a taste for luxury and the habit of spending lavishly as long as the sweat of the peasants could be minted or the Jews cajoled or coerced into lending. It was a period of no common extravagance that included in the list of its follies the Field of the Cloth of Gold, that stupendous pageant, to attend which, in a style befitting their own pride and the vanity of their sovereign, half of the nobles of England were impoverished. It was a glorious period for the king, the mercers, and the Jews.

Contemporaneous with the English company there was another great corporation that became a thorn in the flesh to the Merchants Adventurers. Having its rise upon the continent, it not only competed successfully with the English company for the trade of many European centres, but actually invaded its own domain and became established in the city of London.

The Hansa, or League, commonly known to English-speaking people by the tautological title of the Hanseatic League, has occupied a place in history as unique and almost as large as that of the more modern British East India Company. It was established in the thirteenth century, when several trading towns in northern Germany formed a union for mutual protection in commerce. Out of this union grew in time an association so powerful that it absolutely controlled not only the markets but the government of the cities in which it was principally centred. It obtained, in return for substantial equivalents, letters of protection from some of the principal mercantile cities of the world, notably London, Novgorod, Bergen, Bruges, and Wisby. In each of these cities branches or "factories" for the furtherance of trade were established, and these agencies were under a strict, almost monastic, discipline. The young men employed were unmarried and were required to conduct themselves with the most severe propriety. The London factory was at the steel yards and the employees of the Hansa there were known as the Merchants of the Stilliards.

Such a concession to a foreign company could only have been granted by the English crown in return for a very considerable subsidy. After the death of Henry VIII., the English rivals made a determined effort to oust their foreign rivals, and would have succeeded had not King Edward been heavily indebted to them. Letters of protection, granting monopolies in trade for a consideration, were not a new thing even in the thirteenth century. As early as the eleventh century, London granted such letters to the merchants of Cologne.

Cologne was for many years the principal mercantile city of Europe. With the development of Lübeck arose a rivalry between the two cities and in time this resulted in a coalition of their principal merchants. To the control gained over the Baltic trade by this combination of powers, the Hansa succeeded, adding to it "other spheres of influence."

By the middle of the Fourteenth Century the Hansa controlled a majority of the cities of importance in

Northern Europe, with Lübeck, Cologne, Brunswick, and Danzig as official headquarters. It was an arrogant democracy, an aristocracy of trade, an anomalous condition under which, before the traditions and prejudices of a feudal system were dead, pride of birth and position was confronted by a new-born pride of wealth. The merchant proclaimed himself the peer of the princeling. His kind styled themselves " Burghers of the Free Towns," as proudly as the courtiers of Francis boasted themselves peers of France. The towns included in the Hansa gave laws to the rest of Europe and nearly every crown in Christendom was glad to buy their friendship.

They waged war with kings and forced markets at the point of the sword. When King Eric of Denmark granted the League exclusive privileges to trade in his dominions he did so under compulsion, the Hansa having declared war. Waldemar IV. also perforce signed a treaty stipulating that no future aspirant for the crown of Denmark could be authorized without the consent of the seventy-seven " Hansen," or towns included in the League.

The Hansen raised armies, set fleets afloat with warlike armaments to interfere with the commerce of other states and other companies, claimed for themselves imperial power both on land and sea, and became one of the important political factors of Europe. The League was at its zenith in the fifteenth century. While in power it did much to extend to distant zones the influence of European civilisation, notably on the

German Ocean and in Russia. Its influence upon the operation of public works, particularly upon the construction of canals, was immeasurable. The proud merchants of the League became the patrons of art, as those of Venice had been, and as those of America seem destined to become.

In time, a time nearly consonant with the discovery in America of a new field for commercial enterprise, the Hansa began rapidly to decline. It had arrogated power that finally arrayed against it the jealous monarchies of the Old World. From the magnificent epoch of its prime to the close of its political power and the curtailment of its commercial supremacy, the interval was startlingly brief. It had been centuries in developing and finally, like a great tree, spread its branches over Northern Europe. The axe was laid to its root when it insolently assumed sovereign power in the states to which its chapters owed allegiance. It was one thing for the German Hansen to make war against Denmark or to dictate terms to a Muscovy grand duke, but it was quite another matter for them to make land grants, to pronounce sentence of outlawry, and even to issue a conscription or call to arms in contravention to the authority of the nominal sovereign under whose jurisdiction they lived. The assumption of authority embracing the "greater and lesser ban " was an usurpation of royal prerogative not to be tolerated even by the royal debtors of the League.

Laws for the government of trade, which form perhaps the earliest complete maritime code ever adopted,

were promulgated by the Hansen towards the end
of the League's supremacy. These Hanseatic laws
became the basis for later customs and a reminder of
them may be found in many of the trade regulations
of modern countries.

The consistent though short-sighted policy of the
Hansa, by which foreign merchants trading with the
free towns were obliged to pay enormous duties, led to
retaliatory measures on the part of the Merchants
Adventurers in England. Though their remonstrances
had failed when addressed to Edward, with Elizabeth
they had more weight. That estimable queen, who
loved her mariners above anything else in her realm,
who esteemed a Merchant Adventurer as highly as a
lord, and held an explorer in greater honour than a
peer, lent a willing ear to the expostulations of the
London Mercers and expelled the merchants of the
Stilliards, bag and baggage, from their long-established
headquarters. Not content with mere expulsion she
despatched Drake and a fleet with orders to destroy the
shipping of the Hansa upon the high seas, wherever
met.

The difficulty was finally compromised and the
Hansards re-established in their old seat ; but the
power of the League was broken and heavy duties
were imposed upon its goods in London, where formerly it had enjoyed the greatest privileges.

The readjustment following the decline of the League
and the distribution of its extensive trade led to the
formation of new companies. The expulsion of the

Flemish merchants from their own land opened a way for the concentration of great financial interests and powerful mercantile influences in Amsterdam. The waning power of the Hansa was appropriated by the newly organised East India Company of the Netherlands, while at nearly the same time the Russia or Muscovy Company took to itself the paramount influence of the Merchants Adventurers of England.

In Holland several minor companies consolidated under the title of the East India Company, the West India Company, for many years the arbiter of the fortunes of New Netherland, being subsequently organised. It was the East India Company with which Hudson contracted before setting out on his third and most important voyage, and the West India Company, organised in 1614, that colonised the land that he explored, from the Island of Manhattan to the head of navigation upon the Hudson River.

This brief sketch of the powerful associations that controlled the trade of Northern Europe and Britain for several centuries is a necessary prelude to the story of the great commercial operations of the seventeenth century. The mercantile traditions of the time were an inheritance from an earlier epoch. The ambitious projects of the Dutch East India Company and the English Muscovy Company were not without notable precedent. Parallel with the genealogies of kings and the relation of dynasties run the broad lines of mercantile succession.

Inseparable from the very genius of the Muscovy

Company was the idea of a northern passage to the Eastern ocean, to the lands whence came spices, pearls, and rare objects of merchandise, and it is known that Sebastian Cabot was one of the earliest if not the very first mariner to suggest and attempt that short cut to the Mecca of all merchants. As already intimated, he was largely instrumental in forming the Muscovy Company, which was established when he was an old man, nearly half a century after his first voyage in search of that passage. The Cabots, though the father was Genoese by birth, were English by adoption. Their achievements afforded a wonderful stimulus to nautical adventure and they may justly be regarded as the fathers of the modern English maritime spirit.

While it may be admitted that Sebastian Cabot's accounts of his discoveries were not always exact in detail, yet he was certainly the first navigator of whom the world has knowledge to determine that North America was a new and unexplored continent. His first voyage did not open his eyes to the fact that the land he had touched, and which he called Newfoundland, was other than the coast of Asia, but when, in 1498, he visited those bleak shores the second time he discovered his error. He was among the first, if not the very first, to depict upon his charts a continuous continental coast line from Labrador to Florida.

Next to the Cabots in point of time we find mentioned the Sieur Beveren, who was a favourite with Charles V. before that great ruler assumed the imperial

crown.   Beveren, like many another man of his day,
was paid for distinguished loyalty by a cheap and
showy title to lands of which the very existence was
open to doubt.   The tenure of such grants was uncertain, but often carried with it empty honours.   Sieur
Beveren despatched in search of a certain island, or an
uncertain island, somewhere upon the coast of the
new continent, an expedition consisting of the first
Dutch ships that ever crossed the Atlantic. He accomplished nothing of importance save that he marked a
way by which others were not slow to follow.   Within
a few years a number of sailors from the Low Countries
are supposed to have cruised in the same direction, and
it is more than possible that some of them may have
entered the very waters that Hudson subsequently
explored.

The most prominent of the contestants for the honour
of discovering the Hudson River was a Florentine
named Giovanni da Verazzano, sailing in the French
service.   His first voyage was undertaken about the
year 1508, from Dieppe, in company with Master
Thomas Aubert, who we are told was the son of the
Viscount of Dieppe.   These two made some notable explorations, entering the mouth of the St. Lawrence
River and sailing inland on that stream "upward of
eighty leagues "; the name of St. Lawrence was given
to the river because it was upon that saint's natal day
that they began their ascent of its waters.   Returning
to France they took with them several of the savage
inhabitants of the new country and entertained their

patrons with glowing accounts of the fertility of the land they had seen and the lucrative trade in pelfries that they foresaw.

A second time, fourteen years later than the voyage just mentioned, Verazzano again set sail for the Western continent. This time he was selected by that astute judge of men Francis I. to accomplish for France what it was evident that his neighbours, north and south would not long leave undone. The Portuguese were particularly active in exploration, under the leadership of King John III., and it is told that the Florentine went to Francis with a direct offer to discover kingdoms in the East which the Portuguese had not found. This bold promise was soon repeated to King John, and while Francis, accepting his opportunity, was making ready to despatch Verazzano with a fleet from one of the ports of Normandy, a Portuguese envoy named Joao da Silveyra was posting to France to put what obstructions he could in the mariner's way.

Spite of obstacles the Florentine got away late in 1523 with four ships, all of which, however, returned in a little while disabled. After a few months Verazzano was again on the ocean, this time in *La Dauphine*, bent upon the prosecution of his enterprise. Fortune favoured him and he returned to Normandy in the midsummer of 1524, bringing to the King a journal of his adventures and a chart, both of which have become famous because of long controversy. Verazzano's journal is too long for insertion here, yet too important to be omitted from the present work; it will therefore be given with certain similar addenda at the end of this volume.

It has been the opinion of Professor John Fiske and of other historians that Verazzano did actually discover and enter the bay of New York eighty-five years before the *Half Moon* sailed in the same waters. How far he penetrated cannot be determined, but, while his exploration of the coast was important to geographers, his discovery of the river was not accompanied by thorough exploration nor followed by any attempt at colonisation, so that it was of practically no value to the people of his generation.

Verazzano's earlier voyage, in which he showed the way to the St. Lawrence River, was more productive of results. From that region, which for many years bore the name of New France, it is quite possible that adventurous French traders journeyed *down* the Hudson in their boats or canoes and even made some attempt to trade before Hudson entered the Narrows. There are also some suggestive indications, but not amounting to historic proof, that French trading sloops had visited Hudson's river before the arrival of the *Half Moon*. A Hollander understood some Indians to say so, and engraved the information upon the margin of a map that was made in 1614. Equally vague are other statements bearing upon the same assumption. There is no evidence that Hudson was acquainted with the journal or the map of Verazzano or of any other who preceded him through the beautiful bay of New

York or past the wonderful wall of the Palisades. It would make no difference in our estimate of the importance of his work if we had such proof.

Besides the French there were Spanish and Portuguese navigators to whom mention must be accorded in this connection. One Estevan Gomez, who sailed as chief pilot with Magellan in 1519, is supposed to have explored the North American coast in the early part of the sixteenth century. Peter Martyr is quoted as an authority for the statement that Gomez visited the Hudson River, and the testimony on this point is almost convincing. Gomez describes a bay which he calls St. Christabel, and a river that he names St. Antonio. Certain writers believe that these were none other than Raritan Bay and the Hudson River. The utmost that we can say in regard to this claim is that it is probably correct, but not absolutely proven.

Van der Donck, whose history of New Netherland has been frequently and justly discredited, makes this admission: "There are some who maintain that the Spaniards were in this country many years before, but finding it so cold left it, but I could never so understand it." We are assured by some of those who have made a careful study of the evidence relating to the pre-Hudsonian discovery of the river that the Rio De Montaigns, the Rio San Antonio of Gomez, the Grandissima Riviera of Verazzano, and the Mauritius River of the Hollanders were one and the same stream.

Of all the adventurous navigators of the sixteenth century the Dutch were among the most prominent, and no mariners, even in Holland, were held in greater esteem than Jacob Heemskirk and Willem Barentz or Barentzoon. These men commanded a little fleet that towards the end of the sixteenth century was fitted out by some Amsterdam merchants with the purpose of sailing north across the frozen zone to the rich lands on the other side of the world. Their purpose was the same which afterward animated Hudson, and their adventures and discoveries were well known to him. Failing to accomplish their aim they returned to Amsterdam, where for a time they seem to have remained inactive, though Heemskirk afterwards associated with himself Jan Cornelissen Ryp, also of Amsterdam, and together they made another dash for the polar sea. This was the same Heemskirk who subsequently became well known as a naval commander and lost his life in the service of his native country.

He and Cornelissen sailed in two vessels from Amsterdam in 1596, and sought a north-western passage to China, but, failing to find it, separated at Beeren Island, from which point Cornelissen returned to Amsterdam. Heemskirk then tried the north-east and reached the Nova Zembla coast, where he was caught in ice and compelled to spend the winter, suffering great hardships, but finally succeeded in returning home. The reports made by Cornelissen and Heemskirk effectually chilled for the time whatever hope the Hollanders entertained of finding a passage to China by the north.

Another Cornelissen, namely Jan Cornelissen Leyen,

of Enckhuysen, was engaged about 1597, with an alderman in Amsterdam named Gerret Bikker, in furnishing some vessels for the purpose of exploring the Arctic channels, but whether or not to find a passage to Cathay we do not know. The following year the Hollanders sent some vessels to the West Indies to trade or pillage. It is said that some of these ships, in the employ of the Greenland Company, made a shelter or fort on the coast that was afterwards known as New Netherland, not with any purpose of colonisation, but simply to have a place of refuge during the winter months. There is a very interesting and valuable document bearing upon this subject, drawn up in the form of a report, from papers placed in the hands of a special committee by the Dutch East India Company, and dated the 15th December, 1644. The preamble or introductory paragraph is as follows: " New Netherland, situate in America between English Virginia and New England; extending from the South River, lying in thirty-eight and one half degrees to Cape Malabar, in the latitude of forty-one and one half degrees; was first frequented by the inhabitants of this country [*i. e.* Holland] in the year 1598, and established by those of the Greenland Company; but without making any fixed settlements, only as a shelter in the winter: for which purpose they erected there two little forts near the South and North Rivers, against the incursions of the Indians. A charter was afterwards, on the 11th October, 1614, granted by their High Mightiness to Gerrit Jacobsz Wittsen (and others) to trade exclusively

to the newly discovered lands now called New Netherland, etc.

As every scholar must concede, this testimony, translated from documents preserved in the archives of the
company that employed Henry Hudson, has convincing
weight. It should be observed that in it no mention is
made of our navigator. In the account published by
Hessel Gerritz the same omission is elsewhere noted.
The North and South rivers of New Netherland mean
the Hudson River and the Delaware. These terms
were never applied by the Dutch to any other streams
upon the American continent. If we should leave out
every other claim of discovery, even that of Verazzano,
there seems to be enough here to challenge Hudson's
title as the first discoverer of the river that bears his
name.

Those whose exploits we have so far considered were
foreigners who with the single exception of Sebastian
Cabot probably exerted no direct influence upon the
character, ideals, and life of our navigator. Let us
turn for a while to a consideration of some of the more
prominent English mariners who were the immediate
forerunners of Hudson, and try to understand what
manner of men they were who literally turned the
world upside down.

Davis, Frobisher, Sir Humphrey Gilbert, Sir Walter
Raleigh, Drake, Hawkins, and a score of others are
among the most familiar names of English history.
Their very title suggests a sort of golden age among
seafaring men, when the man who trod a quarter-deck

was a welcome visitor in the halls of nobles and even in the palaces of royalty. Raleigh was the courtier of Elizabeth, yet he was no less a sailor, a commander of expeditions, the discoverer of Guiana, and the fighter of battles on the high seas. Frobisher was knighted for his services and his discoveries. Hawkins commanded fleets, overcame Spanish argosies, captured bullion, traded in slaves, divided his spoils with his sovereign, and commanded her favour and esteem.

Somewhere in Yorkshire—probably at Doncaster— Martin Frobisher was born, about 1535. Date and place are both uncertain. He sailed in most of the waters "underneath the line" till the middle of the century, when, having gained the notice and favour of Elizabeth, she suggested to the Muscovy Company that he be commissioned to search for a north-western passage to that market which was exciting the world's rivalry. He made the attempt in two vessels in the year 1576. It was in some respects rather a feeble undertaking if measured by later expeditions, but it will be forever distinguished as the initial voyage of its kind undertaken by Englishmen. Frobisher sighted the north coast of Greenland, which he thought to be the shore set down by the brothers Zeni as Friesland. Then he found a bay that he mistook for a strait and called it after himself. Having spent about two weeks in exploration he returned to England, bringing with him some specimens of ore he had found on an island.

The following year he was placed in command of a

second expedition, better equipped than the first, for
his specimens of ore pleaded potently for him. He was
to return to the shores he had already visited and
search for gold ; at least, if such was not the tenor of
his instructions, that was what he did. His discoveries at that time were not of particular value and
some of them are in question to this day.

In a third voyage, during which he commanded
fifteen ships, Frobisher discovered the strait through
which Hudson afterwards passed to the great bay that
bears his name, but the channel was not then explored.
The knighting of Martin Frobisher was occasioned by
his services in the fight with the Spanish Armada in
1588, as he proved himself much more admirable as
a warrior than as an explorer. He served with distinction under Drake, and died from the effect of a
wound received in battle.

The names of Frobisher and Davis are usually mentioned in a breath by those who would recount the
maritime glories of England. John Davis was among
the first to make the English mariner familiar with the
stress and peril of arctic voyages, Martin Frobisher
being his only great predecessor. He made three
voyages to the North—the first in 1585 and the last in
1588. His object was to find the north-west passage.
He discovered in his first voyage the strait that bears
his name, and explored portions of the Greenland and
American coasts. Davis wrote several works that
were widely studied in his day and no doubt influenced the thought and activities of merchants as well

as sailors. He was the author of a hydrographical description of the world, and the *Seaman's Secrets* both of which have been republished within the past half-century. Davis lost his life in a fight with Japanese pirates near Malacca only four years before Henry Hudson sailed from Amsterdam in the *Half Moon*. He should not be confounded with John Davis of Limehouse, who was another English sailor-author, but who has nothing to do with this history.

Next to Davis in the mariner's temple of fame perhaps Raleigh may justly claim his place. Edmund Gosse once spoke of Sir Walter Raleigh as "that Paladin of geographical romance," and added : "It is a remarkable tribute to the force and genius of Raleigh that he was recognised in his own age and has been vaunted ever since as the patron as well as the prototype of geography as a form of imaginative literature. In the popular mind, to this day, he gets credit for what he planned to do as well as for what he did. So pertinacious is the legend that connects him with Virginia that I doubt if every one even in this learned assembly [Mr. Gosse was addressing the Royal Geographical Society], recollects that Raleigh never set foot in North America."

He did more—he planned and persisted till the colonisation of Virginia was an accomplished fact. As a discoverer and explorer his name must always be associated with "the large, rich, and beautiful empire of Guiana," which he discovered and explored and concerning which he wrote a "relation" in 1596. We are reminded that Raleigh described in his wonderful book on Guiana some marvels that have no place in accepted natural history to-day. He received, no doubt upon hearsay, and set down as sober fact, accounts of men with heads like dogs and others with their eyes in their shoulders. These fictions are to be regretted or enjoyed according to the mental attitude of the reader, along with Hudson's naïve account of the mermaid, but they do not seriously discredit the main facts of his voyages as set down with an evident intent to be truthful.

Raleigh was more than a sailor, more than a mere navigator; he was a man of science, a scholar whose wisdom ripened under the sun of imagination. His service to posterity was not less than the considerable benefit he imparted to his queen and his contemporaries.

The name of Raleigh inevitably suggests that of Sir Humphrey Gilbert, whose name is among the foremost of England's intrepid sailors and who has the peculiar honour of being the founder of the first British colony, the Adam of a new creation of imperial power and dominion. Like his half-brother, Sir Walter Raleigh, he was an Eton boy. Following Frobisher and Davis, he devoted himself to discovery and adventure, and eventually obtained from Elizabeth a charter or commission entitling him to "inhabit and possess at his choice all remote and heathen lands, not in actual possession of any Christian Prince." The Virgin Queen had a way of making large gifts which cost her

nothing, in exchange for very substantial interests.
The last of Sir Humphrey Gilbert's expeditions was
commenced in the summer of 1583, twenty-four years
before Henry Hudson's first recorded voyage, in a ship
that was called *The Ark Raleigh* after Sir Walter
Raleigh. On this adventure Gilbert lost his life, and
was mourned generally throughout England. His
reputation must have been a great incentive to Hudson, who was probably in his early boyhood at the time
of Gilbert's death. That last voyage led Gilbert to
Newfoundland, of which he took possession in the
Queen's name, though it was already claimed by
the crown of France, and upon which he attempted to
found a colony. His death has been commemorated
by Longfellow in a stanza that is familiar to all readers
of English literature, though singularly limping for
one of the most metrical of poets:

> He sat upon the deck,
> The book was in his hand;
> "Do not fear! Heaven is near",
> He said, "by water as by land!"

After Gilbert we come upon a galaxy of lesser stars,
no one of whom seems to present a claim for pre-
eminence. One of the most interesting characters of
the time was that redoubtable sea warrior Sir John
Hawkins, who had the enviable reputation of being
"merciful, apt to forgive, and faithful to his word."
To him and his son Richard are due a number of remarkable voyages, the history of which would overfill

this book. He rose in the confidence of the Queen and Cecil till he became treasurer and comptroller of the navy, where he laboured to put an end to many abuses, and was at once trusted, feared, and hated, as an able and strict administrator and a tireless reformer. Perhaps no man of his day did more for the welfare of the British seaman than Hawkins—the slave-trader ; unless it was his disciple and friend Drake—the freebooter. This daring mariner and fighter, also knighted for his enterprise, was such a seaman as the world does not often see. He carried the flag of England into the Pacific, and incidentally brought back great treasures that he wrested from the Spaniards.

It was a day when all doors were open to the sailor and all honours and emoluments might be his. We find in the histories of some of the voyages of the time a very startling discrepancy between the religious belief and pious expressions of the English navigators and many of their actions. For example, Drake, who had a chaplain on his vessel during his expedition to the Pacific, and who excommunicated him for attempted mutiny, engaged in enterprises that are not distinguishable from buccaneering. Sir John Hawkins carried slaves from Guinea with such profit to himself and his royal patroness that the Queen allowed him a " demi-moor bound and shackeled " upon his crest ; yet when saved from shipwreck, with a cargo of slaves fettered in the hold of his vessel, he wrote that "God who worketh all things for the best would not have it so, and by him we escaped out of danger." At another time he celebrates a deliverance in these terms : " Almighty God, who never suffereth his elect to perish, sent us on the sixteenth of February the ordinary breeze," etc.

Judged by twentieth-century standards such acts and expressions would stamp any man as an arch-hypocrite, but it is only fair to remember that in the age of Hawkins and Drake, of Cavendish and Hudson, reprisals against the Spaniards were accounted a virtue, and no one had preached or had even imagined the iniquity of a trade in which nearly all nations engaged. The religious sentiments of the sixteenth century sailors, though often crude, were in the main probably sincere.

If the character of the master-mariners of that day were, as has been indicated, not inferior to the landsman of superior rank, it will be interesting to consider what sort of men sailed before the mast. In the first place let it be said that it is by no means assured that most of those who attained eminence as seamen were not first ordinary sailors before the mast. We know that the pirates and buccaneers of a later day were themselves of the rifraff of creation and that they commanded men no better than themselves and certainly no worse. In fact the Portugue or Morgan type of freebooter and their crews were criminals and outlaws, the offscouring of Christendom ; but we have no reason to suppose that the ordinary English seamen of the times of Elizabeth and James I. were generally men of rough or forbidding character.

As already suggested there is good evidence to indicate that the Russia or Muscovy Company chose young men of respectable and in some cases eminent families, to educate them by actual service for the higher duties that they might afterward be called upon to perform. We may suppose Henry Hudson to have been so trained. We find that of the journals and records upon which we must depend for an account of his voyages three at least were written by members of his crews upon successive voyages. We find a mate, Juet, and two common sailors, Pleyce and Prickett, not only able to write but to write English equal to that of many a statesman or professional man of their day.

The name of Humfrey Gilby appears in the list of Hudson's sailors. It has been suggested that, in view of the facts that orthographic errors were of frequent occurrence at that day, that the sons of distinguished fathers were trained to seamanship by actual service and that both Sir Humphrey Gilbert and Henry Hudson were connected with the Muscovy Company, it is not improbable that the man above referred to was a younger Humphrey Gilbert of the same family as the famous explorer.

No doubt there were adventurers and debtors driven by the cruelty of the English laws to seek exile, and sometimes even criminals were employed upon the expeditions that served to create England's power upon the seas, but I do not believe that the employment of such men was by any means general. The unprecedented growth of England's sea power, the high character of the achievements which distinguished her during the sixteenth and seventeenth centuries, could not have been accomplished by men of inferior character. Rogues and ruffians are not the class to whom we may look for great accomplishments. Hudson seemed unfortunately to have been placed in command of mixed crews, partly Dutch, partly English.

Of the Dutch sailors employed at that period it is difficult to speak with any authority. The accounts of the voyages of Hollandish vessels seem to indicate that their crews were composed of men of rougher mould than the English sailors.

In the preceding pages I have called attention to some of the great trading companies that were pressing outward the bounds of the known world and doing so not less effectively because their motive was not glory, but simply a normal selfishness. A brief list of another class of men, more heroic than the first, but dependent upon them for the means to attempt brilliant enterprises, has also been given. There still remains to be added a word as to some of the influences that contributed to the development and conservation, among the sailors of England and the Continent, of what for want of a better term we may call a professional cult, that permitted an interchange of knowledge on matters pertaining to the general business of a mariner's life, yet did not preclude zealous rivalry when occasion offered.

The first of the great navigators of the period we are studying came from the south of Europe, from Genoa, Naples, Florence, or Venice. The first influence to move the mariners of the North was a foreign one.

Many of the pioneer navigators of Europe were Venetian either by birth or adoption. The "Pride of the Sea," the so-called republic of the Doges, was the cradle and nursery of seamen as of merchants; the home of navigators and explorers, no less than of the luxurious princes of commerce and the patrons of art. At the time of which we are writing the territorial possessions of Venice were in constant jeopardy from jealous neighbours, and her supremacy upon the ocean had received a fatal blow by the discovery of the passage to India by way of the Cape of Good Hope, but her inflence in the political world had not yet sensibly declined, nor was the diminution of her mercantile supremacy apparent. Yet Venice was passing the zenith of her glorious day when the sun of England and of Holland was still ascending, though her influence in the mart and upon the broad domain of the sea was still immeasurable. London, Antwerp, and Amsterdam learned their earliest lessons of maritime control from the great mistress of that art, the most serene city of Saint Mark.

In the sixteenth and seventeenth centuries navigators and geographers formed a class by themselves. In spite of jealousies born of a natural rivalry there was a freemasonry between navigators and the chroniclers of their voyages. While the great trading companies guarded whatever information they possessed concerning coasts or continents, as part of assets, the seamen in their employ seem to have exercised a more catholic view of their work, and frequently shared with each other the information gained at the hazard of their lives.

So we read that Boty the Icelander wrote a treatise that fell into the hands of Barentz, from whom Hondius had it, and lent it to Hudson. Barentsen and Heemskirk, as we have seen, associated with Cornelissen, and their log-book came finally into the custody of Hakluyt. Hudson, the disciple of Davis and the friend of John Smith, was also a friend of Hakluyt, and no doubt received from the latter full information concerning the voyages of the Dutch navigators. There seems to have been an endless chain connecting all the northern mariners and the map-makers.

When Henry Hudson appeared before the merchants of Amsterdam, Mercator the geographer, the "cosmographer" of Julich and Cleves, had been dead fifteen years. The projection of meridian parallels, by which his name is widely known to-day, had already come into general use among cartographers in 1609. His latest maps indicated with more or less accuracy the position of certain prominent coastal features upon that great continent to which Columbus had unwittingly opened the way, which the Cabots knew, but recognised only as a troublesome barrier interposed between Europe and the far East. Mercator's last work, completed after he had passed his eightieth year, was the precious *Atlas* that shocked the ecclesiastical power at Rome and was placed upon the index by the scandalised theologians. Mecator was among the very earliest of modern cartographers. The system of map-making which first became familiar through his work and that of his cotemporaries originated about the middle of the sixteenth century.

Closely related to the phenomenal activity that distinguished navigation and commerce in that age was the widespread interest in the position of cities, mountains, forests, and waterways, and the contour of coast lines. Of map-makers there were many in Mercator's time, while the more accurate and more difficult art of producing marine charts was in the hands of a few picked men. An approximately accurate guide would serve the merchant who conveyed his goods under armed escort from town to town, but the navigator, taking larger risks, required a more perfect indication of distances, of the position of rocks and shoals, or the proximity of bays and harbours. Such charts were drawn generally from the reports, descriptions, and sketches of mariners, and in successive editions were corrected as new data were furnished. The cartographer held a semi-official position in most European countries and his work had the highest authority. In Spain and Portugal great secrecy was maintained by those who produced and by those who used the precious charts, for it was held, not unreasonably, that something of the maritime and commercial supremacy of those countries was due to the exclusive character of much of their knowledge respecting distant coasts and the routes by which they could be safely reached. To a lesser degree this jealous custom of guarding a chart as a possession not to be shared by a foreigner obtained in all countries and often defeated its own selfish end. Scrutiny of the charts of that period will convince the student that the navigators of one nationality sometimes persisted for years in errors which those of other countries had long abandoned.

There is good evidence that Henry Hudson used a chart prepared by Jodicus Hondius, and the mistakes that Hondius made, mistakes that were not by any means original with him, were no doubt a direct cause of Hudson's failures, as they were notable among the several inspirations of his erroneous theories.

Upon another page the life and services of Hondius are more particularly treated. In spite of errors which were unavoidable in his day, his influence upon the enterprise and thought of contemporary merchants and mariners was incalculable. To him Holland owed much of the impulse that led to her almost supreme position in maritime affairs. What Holland owed to Hondius, England owed to Richard Hakluyt, the recorder of discoveries and explorations, the careful historian of voyages and the friend of many navigators. He had studied at Westminster School under the mastership of Camden. From him perhaps young Hakluyt derived his early love for globes, maps, and all the paraphernalia of geographical study. His first work after leaving Oxford was to lecture upon that fascinat-

ing theme, and we have his own word for the
fact that he did so "to the great content of his
auditory."

He was among the first to perceive the great need of
a scientific training for seamen, and to realise the importance of collating the records of the voyages for the
information of navigators.   The first of these needs he
tried to satisfy by the establishment of a permanent
lectureship, and his attempt to obviate the second led
to those painstaking researches and voluminous notes
that have made him the most conspicuous among early
geographers.   Hakluyt was in a fever over the results
of the voyages of Hawkins and Drake.   " The naked-
ness of the Spaniards and their long-hidden secrets are
now at length espied," he wrote.   There was a chance
to colonise.   Send " some of our superfluous people
into those temperate and fertile parts of America
which, being within six weeks sailing of England, are
yet unpossessed by any Christians and seem to offer
themselves unto us, and stretching nearer unto Her
Majesty's dominions than to any other part of
Europe."

We are indebted to Samuel Purchas, an English
clergyman of Hudson's time, for most of the information we possess relating to Henry Hudson and his
voyages.   To his vanity or his lack of perception is
due the incalculable loss of much of the material
which Hakluyt did not find time to put into shape
and publish before his death.   The literary remains
of Hakluyt were appropriated, curtailed, garbled, by

Purchas. Yet the latter was himself a writer of indefatigable perseverance and showed at times an intelligent interest in those noble aims to which Hakluyt devoted his life.

CHAPTER II

ITHIN the limits of old London town, not far from the ancient site of Bishop's Gate, stands the church of St. Ethelburga. W. J. Loftie once wrote concerning it that, "because of the comparatively genuine and unsophisticated state of its ancient architectural features, this is one of the most interesting of London churches, even though it contains no magnificent names and is connected, it is my duty to note, with the names of no illustrious men."

The historian of London churches and London streets either overlooked an important historical event or undervalued the achievements of a famous Englishman when he denied to St. Ethelburga's the association of one illustrious name.

Upon the 19th day of April, 1607, into that house of worship passed a little company of twelve English mariners. They were of the same type as those intrepid followers of Drake and Hawkins, of Raleigh and Gilbert, of Frobisher and Cabot, whose unsurpassed seamanship and daring extended the dominion of England and the fame of England's Queen. The leader of these men was one of whose history previous to that day the world has absolutely no record, yet he was destined within the short space of four years to fix his name and personality imperishably upon the page of history. He was to set out upon a voyage which should mean to him great distinction, that was to gain him rating with the foremost explorers of all time. He was to achieve many triumphs, though he accomplished not one of the results for which he hoped. He was to be called a great discoverer, though it has not been actually proved that he made any original territorial discovery. He was sought after by the great leaders of trade in two of the foremost maritime countries of the world, yet never fulfilled their expectations of him. He held, through four successive voyages, his influence over several of those who entered with him into the church of St. Ethelburga, yet he was at last the victim of a senseless and cowardly mutiny.

From the pages of *Purchas his Pilgrimes*, the following account of Hudson and his companions may be quoted: "At St. Ethelburga's in Bishop's Gate Street, did communicate with the rest of the parish these persons, seamen, proposing to go to sea four days after for to discover a passage by the North Pole to Japan and China. First Henry Hudson, master; secondly, William Collins, his mate; thirdly, James Young; fourthly, John Coleman; fifthly, John Cooke; sixthly, James Beuberry; seventhly, James Skrutton;

eighthly, John Pleyce ; ninthly, Thomas Baxter ; tenthly, Richard Day; eleventhly, James Knight; twelfthly, John Hudson, a boy.'' Purchas is incorrect in designating Collins as mate. That rank, according to Hudson's log, belonged to John Coleman.

The fact that Hudson and his companions went to church to receive the sacrament, before setting out upon a voyage of peril, is suggestive of the great change which had come over the spirit of the English people during the reign of Elizabeth. The Bible had become the book of the people ; the general trend of thought and action was towards religious observances. It has been wisely pointed out by the historian of the English people that to the day of her death Queen Elizabeth belonged to the old order, and in her latter years no longer represented the moral feeling of her people. That great queen reached the end of her life even while some of her more adventurous subjects were establishing new colonies, exploring new lands, setting up new standards, and enlarging the boundaries of the British world. At the time when Hudson first appeared upon the page of history James I. had occupied the throne for three years ; but the spirit that animated Hudson, in common with other adventurous Englishmen, was the spirit of Elizabeth.

We have no authentic likeness of Henry Hudson. The various alleged portraits of him which have been published are purely products of the imagination, their chief value being that they show in appropriate costume a typical mariner of his time. Of Francis Drake,

Sir John Hawkins, and several other eminent seamen of that day, we have more or less accurate likenesses, and it would be fortunate could we discover some picture which might show with certainty how that man appeared whose name is perhaps more familiar to Americans than that of any of the great seamen of his day.

Our ignorance of Hudson's early life is as complete as is our ignorance of his personal appearance. From the fact that one Henry Hudson of an earlier generation was prominent as a founder of the "Muscovy" Company, and as the names of several other Hudsons appear either as directors of that company, captains in its employ, or confidential agents working for its interest in Russia, it has been surmised that the famous Henry Hudson was of the same family as the others, and it is supposed that he may have been the grandson of his earlier namesake. That he was married is a fact established by a certain clause in his contract with the Dutch East India Company. He had at least one son, John, who first appears with him at the church of St. Ethelburga, and finally shares his tragic fate. What other children he may have had we do not know. There is evidence that he numbered among his friends some of the abler men of his day, particularly such as interested themselves in the exploration of new countries.

The service at which we have seen Henry Hudson and his companions was the simpler communion which under the sway of Protestantism in England had everywhere superseded the gorgeous ritual of Rome. The dim light that filtered through the lancet windows of old St. Ethelburga's no longer fell upon resplendent vestments nor was eclipsed by the radiance of clustered candles around a blazing altar. Instead, the communicants, already showing in their sombre attire the soberer tendency of their generation, bowed their heads to repeat with their minister words which they could every one understand. In that little sanctuary, for it was tiny compared with many a modern chapel, among those who broke hallowed bread with Henry Hudson were some who at a later date should raise their hands against his life.

When Hudson stepped from the dark doorway of the mean little building, he appeared not only in the full light of day—a brighter day, we may imagine, than modern London often knows—but came into the focusing rays of historic investigation. Four days later, at Gravesend on the Thames, he embarked for the icy northern seas.

It was a May day when Hudson set sail from Gravesend. The gardens of Kent were commencing to bloom—"drowsy Kent" it has been called, even in our time; the hawthorn was white in the hedgerows and roses were beginning to blossom in the cottage gardens. Here and there a May-pole on some village green, or a band of youthful revellers by the river-side, must have attracted the attention and lured the hearts of the more youthful sailors of the *Hopewell*. As the little vessel dropped down the widening stream, the air was full of spring, and to the master the prospect of his life was full of hope. The accomplishment of his purpose would lead him away from the level green meadows and the flowery gardens of the Thames into the regions of perpetual winter ; but beyond them he saw the wonderful mirage of his day, the lands that were sweet with spices and fruits, and rich with Oriental treasures, abundant and precious beyond comprehension. " Farthest Inde " was the *ignis fatuus* of nearly three centuries, and the polar passage to it was the fatal dream of generations of navigators. An old writer, in a book pretending to give " a true account of the Moscovie or Russian company," stated that when Hudson sailed in the *Hopewell* his object was to discover the North Pole. This was so clearly an error that it seems hardly necessary to refute it.

Clearing the Shoeburyness point and sailing along the shores of Essex and Suffolk, the *Hopewell* left the English coast when off Yarmouth, and taking a northerly direction headed for the Shetland Islands. That group was sighted in twenty-six days, making the average speed of Hudson's vessel during this part of the trip something less than two miles an hour.

While near the Shetland Islands, Hudson noted that he had found the needle to have no variation, but on the 30th of May he discovered that it did " increase 79 degrees under the horizon," and four days later he observed a variation of five degrees westward. The importance of these observations will be realised when it is remembered that he was the first of English navigators to record the dip of the needle, although we can hardly imagine that he was the first to have noticed it.

The course of the *Hopewell* after leaving the Shetland Islands was north-westerly, passing to the north of the Faroe Islands and Iceland, and towards the bleak coast of Greenland. The voyagers were rapidly nearing the arctic circle, but with the approach of the short northern summer, in almost perpetual sunlight, and under the influence of favourable currents, the voyage at that stage could hardly have seemed more arduous than a holiday excursion. The rate of sailing, too, was much more rapid than when going north during the first twenty-six days. In spite of the high latitude the air was almost balmy, as it frequently is to this day in the neighbourhood of the Faroe group.

This smooth sailing was enlivened by occasional minor discoveries that the master thought worth recording. For example, on the eleventh day of June, fifteen days out from the Shetland Islands, six or seven whales were noticed. These swam near the ship and were evidently unconscious of the fact that the little *Hopewell* was only the forerunner of other ships that should, for the space of three centuries, come to wage special warfare against their race.

There occurred a sudden change in the fortunes of Hudson and his crew after passing the open sea between Iceland and Jan Mayen Island. They found their way impeded by ice, the air was thick with a piercing cold

fog, and when that lifted they imagined they saw looming before them a forbidding, gloomy coast. Early
upon the morning of the 13th of June the presence of land became a certainty, though still partly
obscured by the fog. The weather was now so cold
that the decks of the *Hopewell* were coated with ice, and
her rigging and sails rigid with it. The wind blew
from the north-east, rising to a gale; and fearing for the
safety of his vessel Hudson was obliged to run south
eighteen or twenty miles. In the morning the fog had
blown over and he saw land for the first time so dis-
tinctly that he could get an idea of its nature, and estimate the trend of the coast line. The real aspect of the
land was not less bleak and forbidding than imagination had pictured it while it was still half veiled by the
mist.

Hudson wrote in his journal: "This was very high
land, most part covered with snow, the nether part was
uncovered. At the top it looked reddish, and underneath a blackish clay, with much ice lying about it."
The general direction of the land to the northward was
north-east by north. Modern explorers have agreed
that the point discovered by Hudson lay just north of
King Oscar Fjord.

The avowed purpose of the voyage, which was to sail
more directly towards the pole in search of the hoped-
for passage, was departed from in going as far westward
as the Greenland coast. Hudson must have recognised
the fact that his course might have been open to criticism, for he went to the trouble of explaining, by the

way of apology, that he was moved by a strong desire
to see the land about which explorers had given imperfect reports, and desired to add new discoveries to those
already made. In the words of his journal, "Considering we found lands contrary to those our cards
make mention of, we counted our labour so much the
more worthy, and for ought that we could see it is like
to be a good land and worth the seeing."

It will be evident as we advance in the narrative of
Hudson's voyages that this was not the only occasion
upon which he deviated from the letter of his sailing
directions. Some of his biographers have charged him
with disobedience of orders; but this seems to be a
harsh view to take of the matter, since a broad discretion must always be allowed to the navigator who is
exploring strange seas and should in the nature of
things be governed in his actions by many circumstances that his employers could not possibly foresee.

Henry R. Cleveland, writing a generation ago, commenced his sketch of the life of Hudson with a paragraph which describes the qualities of the class of men
to which the subject of the biography belonged :

> In few men are more rare combinations of
> talent required than in discoverers of new countries
> and seas. Invincible courage, patience and forti-
> tude under suffering, daring, enterprise tempered
> by prudence, promptness and decision united with
> calm reflection, sagacity, fertility of invention,
> strong common-sense combined with enthusiasm
> and vivid imagination, the power of commanding
> other minds, joined to gentleness of manner and

ready sympathy, are some of the more prominent traits in the character of this class of men.

Then follows the application: "Among those who were most gifted in these attributes was the subject of the present memoir, Henry Hudson, the bold navigator of the arctic seas."

The first of the *Hopewell's* crew to discover land on the Greenland coast was James Young, and in his honour, with a view no doubt to encourage his men to special vigilance, the master named the first land they saw Young's Cape. Young is assured of geographical immortality, for his name is still to be found on the chart of the Greenland coast. A high hill, described in the journal as "a very high mount, like a round castle," was named "The Mount of God's Mercy." The shore at this point was observed to be the habitat of many birds, and whales were again seen in the vicinity of the *Hopewell*.

It is a matter of surprise that Hudson came so near to the land without being encumbered by the shore ice, which at that season of the year has been found by later voyagers to form a dangerous field, extending its irregular margin many leagues from the coast. For example, the *Antarctic* in the course of the North-east Greenland expedition, in 1899, found the margin of land ice, in July, from twenty to thirty miles outside of the point now called Cape Young.

Leaving the neighbourhood of this cape, the explorer steered in a north-easterly direction, finding, however, that almost every day brought new difficulties and dangers. The fogs that settled over the water, depressing and menacing as they were, were only the alternative of fierce gales, and tried the seamanship of the sailor, and the staunchness of his cockle-shell of a vessel.

Hudson was bent upon exploring that part of the coast for the particular reason that he was not by any means sure whether he had really seen the mainland of Greenland or was merely skirting an island, the shore line of which might presently run away to the westward.

Of the 11th July he wrote :

> Very clear weather, with the wind at south south-east ; we were come out of the blue sea into our green sea again, where we saw whales. Now, having a fresh gale of wind at south south-east, it behooves me to change my course and to sail to the north-east, by the souther end of Newland, but being come into a green sea, praying God to direct me, I steered away north ten leagues. After that we saw ice on our larboard we steered away northward by east three leagues and left the ice behind us. Then we steered away north till noon.
>
> At ten this evening clear weather, and then we had the company of our troublesome neighbours, ice with fog. Here we saw plenty of seals, and we supposed bears had been there by their footing and dung upon the ice. This day many of my company were sick with eating of bear's flesh the day before unsalted.

At last, however, the search for an open sea to the north-west had to be abandoned, owing to the increasing prevalance of ice, and the almost continuous fog. The explorer now changed his course to the north-east so as to make Spitzbergen or Newland. It has been claimed for nearly three centuries that Hudson discovered Spitzbergen, but that claim is entirely without foundation. There seems to be every reason to suppose that he knew of the existence of the group, and that his turning towards it at this time was not merely accidental.

Hudson's knowledge of the trend of the Greenland coast was to be further enlarged before he succeeded in leaving it. He sailed sixty or seventy miles, according to his reckoning, when the look-out saw land on the larboard, or, as we would say, the port side. This unexpected landfall, we are told, was first seen at a distance of about twelve leagues. It was lofty, as indeed it must needs have been to be observed at such a distance, and was covered with snow. Still further north, beyond the coast range, were seen looming the white tops of very high mountains. The explorer reported the weather in this locality as much less severe than that they had experienced, but contented himself with viewing the coast from a distance, and naming it at long range "The Land of Hold with Hope."

Once more before turning more directly to the eastward Coleman, the mate, again saw high land on the port side, and this was the last of the Greenland coast that appeared to those on the *Hopewell* until after their visit to Spitzbergen, towards which they directed their course. Pleyce reports that in this high latitude the sun was now above the horizon during the whole of the twenty-four hours. We also read that the mists and fogs which had so delayed them for a time disappeared, and that they saw flocks of birds similar to those they had noticed upon the Greenland coast.

For the only detailed account of Hudson's voyage in 1607 we must turn to the journal of John Pleyce, who had access to Hudson's log and who copied extracts from it, besides adding much matter of his own. Pleyce was one of the ship's company on board the *Hopewell*, and so far as we know he was no more than a common seaman, yet the journal is written in a style that betokens a fair amount of education. It has been pointed out by Sir Martin Conway that in some respects, either through ignorance of facts or a desire to show more discoveries than Hudson actually made, Pleyce was sometimes inaccurate. The discovery of Spitzbergen is now credited by most geographers to Barentz, and it is not probable that any part of that land was first seen by Hudson. Some of Pleyce's observations, however, are not only interesting but valuable.

On the 27th of June, "about one or two of the clock in the morning," wrote the mariner scribe, "we made Newland [Spitzbergen], being clear weather on sea, but the land was covered with fog, the ice lying very thick all along the coast for fifteen or sixteen leagues, which we saw. Having a fair wind we coasted it in a very pleasing smooth sea, and had no ground at one hundred fathoms, four leagues from shore. This day at noon we were in seventy-eight degrees and we stood along the shore." Then follows a less favourable entry : "This day was so foggy that we were hardly able to see the land many times, but by our account we were near Vogel Hook." Hudson tried thence to shape his course north-westerly, to get away from the land, but was continually driven back by ice, which by midnight of the 28th nearly enclosed his ship, there being great quanties of it between the *Hopewell* and the shore. "By our observation," wrote Pleyce, "we were thwart of the great indraught [*i. e.*, the great Ice Fjord, or *Grooten Inwyck* of Barents]. "To free ourselves of the ice we steered between the southeast and south and to the westward as we could have sea. By six this evening it pleased God to give us clear weather and we found we were shot far into the inlet, being almost a bay and environed with high mountains with lowland between them. We had no ground in this bay at one hundred fathoms." Sir Martin Conway points out that according to Pleyce's account the *Hopewell* could not have been far up the Ice Fjord, as has been sometimes claimed. It "must merely have been somewhat east of the south point of Prince Charles Foreland, but certainly not up Foreland Sound."

Leaving the mouth of the inlet and encountering head winds, drift ice, and bewildering fogs in almost constant succession, Hudson went north, south, or west, as he was able. The record for the 2d of July is a

fair example of the experience through which he had
to pass: "Sailed ten leagues to north-west; it was
searching cold. We also trended the ice, not knowing
whether we were clear or not, the wind being at the
north. The fourth was very cold and our shrouds and
sails frozen; we found we were far in the inlet."
Following this again came more fog, during which the
tide carried the vessel some way up Foreland Sound.
In going back the writer of the journal made note that
near the mouth of the inlet "we strooke a hull,"
which appears to be equivalent to the modern "hove
to."

"Now having the wind north-east," continues the
narrator, "we stood away south and by east with purpose to fall in with the southern-most part of the land
which we saw, hoping by this means either to defray
the charge of the voyage or else, if it pleased God any
time to give us a fair wind to the north-east, to satisfy
expectation." In other words they would consider
that they had accomplished something if they could
discover new land or new parts of the land they had
been coasting, but they hoped ultimately with a favourable wind to be able to prosecute the real object of the
voyage, which was to find a passage to the other side
of the world. The project of sailing southward was
soon abandoned, and on the 11th of June Hudson wrote
in his log, "Having a fresh gale of wind at south
south-east it behooved me to change my course and
sail north-east by the souther end of Newland."
Again the course only ended in ice.

Shortly after this Pleyce makes the following entry in his journal: "At midnight, out of the top William Collins, our boatswain, saw the land called Newland by the Hollanders, bearing south south-west twelve leagues from us." They ran again towards the coast, entering a deep bay, since called Whales Bay, which opens to the west and north, "the bottom and sides thereof being to our sight very ragged and high land." A cape jutting into this bay was called Collins Cape, after the boatswain, who first sighted it. Here occurred one of the most valuable of the observations made by Hudson on the Spitzbergen coast. The bay was full of whales; so full, indeed, that they hampered the ship, and it is probable that Hudson's report of the numbers of cetaceans he found upon the coasts of this island and Greenland was a great stimulus to the whale fishery, which afterwards became so important an industry for English seamen. Pleyce is authority for a remarkable story illustrating the prevalence of whales in the bay: "One of our company having a hook and line overboard to try for fish, a whale came under the keel of our ship and made her held [heel?]; yet by God's mercy we had no harm but the loss of the hook and three parts of the line."

The following description of Whales Bay is evidently copied from Hudson's own account.

At the mouth of this bay we had soundings thirty fathoms and afterwards six and twenty fathoms, but further in we had no ground at one hundred fathoms, and therefore judged it rather a sound than a bay. Between this high ragged land, in the swamps and valleys, lay much snow; here we found it hot. On the souther side of this bay lay three or four small islands or rocks.

In the bottom of this bay, [*i. e.*, at the lower end of the bay] John Coleman, my mate and William Collins, my boatswain, with two others of our company went on shore, and there they found and brought aboard a pair of morse's teeth in the jaw. They likewise found whale's bones and some dozen or more of deer horns. They saw the footings of beasts of other sorts ; they also saw rote geese. They saw much drift-wood on the shore and found a stream or two of fresh water. Here they found it hot on shore and drank water to cool their thirst, which they also commended.

Here, [continues the log], we found the want of a better ship-boat. As they certified me they were not on the shore past half an hour and among other things brought aboard a stone of the country. When they went from us it was calm, but presently after we had a gale of wind at the north-east, which came with fog. We plied to and again in the bay awaiting their coming, but after they came aboard we had the wind at the east and by south, a fine gale. We minding our voyage and the time to perform it [*i. e.*, believing this wind to be favourable], steered away north-east and north north-east. This now proved clear and we had the sun on the meridian on the north and by east part of the compass from the upper end of the horizon. With the cross-staff we found his height ten degrees forty minutes, without allowing anything for the semi-diameter of the sun or the distance of the end of the staff from the center in the eye."

Of part of the coast, easily recognisable as the Seven Icebergs, Pleyce says, "We saw the high part of Newland eighteen or twenty leagues from us to the northeast, being a very high mountainous land like ragged rocks with snow between them."

Hudson seemed frequently to have been out in his reckoning both of distance and of latitude, as all mariners of his day were apt to be, and his estimate of the direction he took was very often at fault. No account of a voyage of discovery down to the latter part of the seventeenth century is to be regarded as entirely trustworthy when it comes to a question of exact locality. Nothing was more common than for two voyagers to discover the same cape or headland or river in apparently different latitudes.

Deceived by his own misconception of the direction of the coast, and miscalculating its probable extent, Hudson

> hoped to have had a free sea between the land and the ice, but now find by proof it was impossible by means of the abundance of ice compassing us about by the north and joining to the land, and seeing God did bless us with a fair wind to sail by the south of this land [*i. e.*, around the south cape] to the north-east, we returned, bearing up the helm, minding to hold to that part of the land which the Hollanders discovered, and, if contrary winds should take us, to harbour there, and try what we could find to the charge

of our voyage, and to proceed with our discovery as soon as God should bless us with
wind. I think this land may be profitable to
those that will venture it. In this bay, before
spoken of [*i. e.*, Whale Bay], and about this coast
we saw more abundance of seals than we had seen
any time before.

By the 25th of July, Hudson abandoned the idea of
exploring the Spitzbergen coast further, and sailed
west for Greenland ; intending after visiting that shore,
where he perhaps hoped to have found the ice and fogs
less prevalent than earlier in the season, "to have
made my return by north of Greenland to Davis his
straits and so for England."

We cannot understand what object the explorer had
in returning to Greenland in order to effect a retreat to
England, the season having advanced so that he knew
that his project of finding a passage through the ice
across the pole must be abandoned. There would
seem to be no further object to be gained in keeping
his ship and ship's company upon a voyage that must
have been tedious and was certainly expensive. We
can only conjecture that the intense curiosity of the
explorer, than which there seems hardly a stronger
passion, prompted him to visit the strait which was
associated with the name of one of his greatest rivals
for fame, and, if possible, to add some new discovery
which should enhance his own reputation.

Before reaching the shores of Greenland Hudson
met with an adventure such as has often proved the

climax and conclusion of an arctic voyage. Caught between two great bodies of ice the little vessel of not more than eighty tons was nearly crushed, her salvation coming with the providential springing up of the wind from such a quarter that it parted the ice, enabling her to escape into more open water. The grinding together of the great fields of floe ice is described as causing a sound like thunder.   Before the wind came to their aid Hudson had the ship's boat overboard and manned in an effort to tow the *Hopewell* out of danger.

The description of this danger as written by the navigator is worth transcription here :

> The seven and twentieth, extreme thick fog— then it was calm and the sea very loftie. We heard a great ruttle or noise with the ice and sea, which was the first ice we heard or saw since we were at Collins Cape, the sea heaving us westward towards the ice. We heaved out our boat and rowed to toe out our ship farther from the danger, which would have been to small purpose by means the sea went so high, but in the extremity it pleased God to give us a small gale at north-west and by west, we steered away southeast, four leagues till noon.   Here we had finished our discovery if the wind had continued that brought us hither, or if it had continued calm. But it pleased God to make this north-west and by west wind the means of our deliverance ; which wind we had not found common upon the voyage. God give us thankful hearts for our so great deliverance.   Here we found the want of a good ship-

> boat, as once we had done before at Whale Bay.
> . . . From four to six, south four leagues and
> found by the icy sky and our nearness to Grone-
> land that there is no passage that way : which if
> there had been I meant to make my return by
> the north of Groneland to Davis his straits and
> so for England.

Shortly after this escape Hudson saw from the appearance of the sky that there could be no passage
such as he hoped to the north of Greenland. It is well
known that under certain conditions the sky reflects
great masses of ice, or of what sailors call white water
(*i. e.*, shoal water). This phenomenon is frequently
observed not only among the ice-fields of the frozen
north, but where the great sandy shallows of the
Bahamas and other southern archipelagoes present a
glistening surface to the sky.

Dr. Asher points out in this connection that Greenland was in Hudson's time too imperfectly known for
him to have understood the impossibility of returning
to England by such a course. "The fact that such
a passage does not exist is one of the most important
geographical results obtained by this expedition."

The navigator now turned in earnest towards home.
In passing near the southern part of Spitzbergen he
saw again in the distance the coast about which he
had been so long driven by contrary winds. One more
discovery he recorded before reaching England, and
that was the island of Jan Mayen, which he named
"Hudson's Touches."

That he had not accomplished the object for which he set out must have been a sore disappointment both to the navigator and his employers, but his reports of what he had seen of the peculiar nature of the coasts he had visited, and the hardships he had overcome, gave him a great reputation and opened the way, no doubt, to his subsequent voyages. We cannot estimate the importance of Hudson's report to those who received it, nor could they with their insufficient knowledge tell how valueless were some of the discoveries upon which he most prided himself.

Hudson passed in clear weather, we are told, within sight of Cheries Island, and had a distinct view of that forbidding, rocky coast. Through the latter days of summer he sailed southward until in the early autumn he arrived at Tilbury Hope on the Thames. The whole exploration had occupied only four and a half months. The last entry in the log of that famous voyage was as follows: "The fifteenth of August we put into the Isles of Faire [Faroe Islands] and on the fifteenth of September I arrived at Tilberie Hope on the Thames."

It will not be out of place to append to this chapter several observations of a curious rather than important character, which may serve to illustrate the foregoing text. During Hudson's struggles to find a clear passage to the north-east of Spitzbergen certain natural phenomena attracted his attention. Among other things he recorded that the ocean varied greatly in colour, at one time appearing blue, at another time green, at another black. The walrus, or, as it was then called, the morse, shared that icy domain with abundant seals and not infrequent bears.

In trying to comprehend the logs of the early explorers great confusion has occurred by reason of the misapplication of names to Greenland and Spitzbergen. The older navigators frequently confounded geographical localities, and often several names were bestowed upon the same body of land or water, while not infrequently the same name was attached to several islands, bays, headlands, or rivers.

Apropos of the Spitzbergen discovery, Hudson left a paper containing memoranda of Barentz's voyage, on the top of which appears in his own hand, "This was written by William Barentson on loose paper and was lent me by the Reverend Peter Plantius in Amsterdam, March the seven and twentieth, 1609."

Dr. Asher, in his introduction to *Henry Hudson, the Navigator*, says:

> As to the real or western Greenland, Hudson designates it by a name nearly identical with the Engroneland of the Zeni chart which, partly copied by Hondius, was probably known and possibly used by Hudson; he called it Groneland. We cannot understand his log-book without bearing in mind that this Groneland is Greenland, while his Greenland is Spitzbergen.

Dr. Asher further says:

> Newland was the name given to Spitzbergen

by several of the Dutch geographers. This the
English afterwards converted into King James—
his Newland. The most general name for the
country was, however, Greenland. The name of
Spitzbergen was invented by Hessel Gerritz, in
1613, possibly on the authority of Barentz.

We must believe that Hudson was frequently unable
to form a clear conception of his whereabouts. In one
place he says: "Being then, as we supposed, in the
meridian of the same land, having no observation
since the eleventh day, and laying a hull [that is,
'laying to'] from the fifteenth to the seventeenth day,
we perceived a current setting to the south-west,"
etc. This was written as part of the record of the 18th
of June.

In reading Hudson's (or Pleyce's) log one cannot but
be struck by the many curious and often archaic expressions that are used to describe familiar nautical
manœuvres. While off Vogel Hook, on the 29th of
June, 1607, we learn that the wind at four o'clock in
the morning was "a pretie gale." In more than one
entry the phrases "lay a hull" and "strooke a hull"
are used in such connection that we may translate them
"lay to" or "hove to." We are informed that on the
25th of July "the wind scanted"—and changed.
"It was searching cold," we are told upon the approach
to the shore of Greenland. To "lay a board" is not
quite comprehensible to the lay reader, nor can he
readily understand what is meant by the words "I

found the sea more growne than any we had since we left England." After all, to the average landsman, sailor's English, even at the present day, is not an open book, and many of the survivals of antique phrases are quite as curious as the obsolete ones here noted.

CHAPTER III

NNO 1608, the two and twentieth of Aprill, being Friday, we set saile at St. Katherines, and fell down to Blackewall."

St. Katherine's docks afterwards marked the spot from which Hudson sailed on his second voyage. He was in the employ of the same company that sent him out in 1607, but now he was to endeavour to find in the north-east what he had failed to discover in the north-west, the passage to China and the Indian Ocean. His plan was to proceed along the Norwegian coast, to round the North Cape, and stand westwardly towards Nova Zembla ; then, skirting the western shore of that island, seek to the north-east of it the passage for which he had vainly searched along the coast of Greenland.

His departure from London was not heroic ; dropping down with the tide he rounded the Isle of Dogs and skirted the famous Greenwich marshes, where in his day the wild fowl still flew from pond to pond, and at nightfall his anchor was cast off Blackwall. The members of Hudson's ship's company on this voyage are to be found in his log, and the list is of proper interest among the meagre records of the expedition.

> Their names employed in this action are as followeth : Henry Hudson, master and pilot ; Robert Juet, the master his mate ; Ludlow Arnall ; John Cooke, boatsonne ; Philip Stacie, carpenter ; John Barnes ; John Braunch, cooke ; John Adrey ; James Strutton ; Michel Feirce ; Thomas Hilles ; Richard Tomson ; Robert Raynor ; John Hudson and Humfrey Gilby.

More than cursory reference should be made to Robert Juet, the master's mate, mentioned in the preceding paragraph. This man, with whom we shall make closer acquaintance, was "an elderly man" and accompanied Hudson upon at least three of his voyages. He wrote the journal upon which we rely for most of our information regarding the third, or Hudson River expedition, and was identified with the mutineers who caused Hudson's death upon the fourth voyage.

One month after the date of his departure from London Hudson wrote, "By observation we were in 64 degrees 52 minutes"; in other words, upon the Norwegian coast. Here he was greatly delayed by inclement weather, and beset by almost continuous fogs ; but after several days the weather somewhat cleared and the navigator's hopes were raised by prospects of fair skies and an open sea.

As the explorer approached the northern end of Norway the increasing cold incapacitated several of the crew, including the ship's carpenter, so that almost at the commencement of the voyage the vessel was short-handed; but the commander showed then, as always during his short career, that superiority to circumstances and disregard of difficulties which was so marked an element of his character. In spite of the indisposition of his crew, and the consequent peril in which the little vessel stood, we find Hudson calmly making observations and noting phenomena. He recorded the appearance of the unsetting sun, being the first of all Englishmen to write that he had taken an observation at midnight. A few extracts from his log may be transcribed without apology to the reader:

The eight and twentieth [of May], drie cold cleere weather; the wind between north north-west and north . . wee saw the sunne on the north meridian above the horizon 5 degrees, 35 minutes. . . . The First of June, a hard gale at east northeast, with snow; we made our way good south southeast. The second a hard gale of wind at northeast; toward night, calm with fogge, our course was southeast all day. The third in the morning we had a sight of the North Cape [the most northern part of Norway] . . observing the variation I found it to the westward 11 degrees, and having a smooth sea, the needle inclined under the horizon 84 degrees and a half, the nearest I could finde. It was cleere weather, and we saw Norway fishermen at sea.

The *fourth*, warme clear sunshine. Now by God's help the carpenter recovered, and made a mast for our ship's boat and the companie made a sayle.

So the log runs, great things and small being

jumbled together, as has been the fashion with logs since the Muscovy Company, that employed Hudson, first instituted their use.

The navigator now approached the coast of Nova Zembla, where for the first time upon this voyage he found his way obstructed by ice. He tried to force his vessel through the treacherous, shifting barrier, but the ice closed in about him, battering his vessel and so endangering it that a retreat was necessary. Several subsequent efforts were made to accomplish a passage to the north or north-east, but in every case the trial was unavailing.

The vessel was on soundings almost daily. Hudson reports that the water was a whitish-green, and that great numbers of whales were sighted, while flocks of sea-fowl covered the face of the ocean. On the ice that surrounded them the crew could hear the roaring of numerous bears, and seals appeared in abundance. Not only did these wonders of natural history appeal to the men under Hudson's command, but still greater marvels were recorded as having been seen by them. Two of the sailors—whose names should be forever immortalised—Thomas Hils, or Hillis, and Robert Raynor, gravely reported to the master, and he as gravely noted in his log, that while looking over the side of the ship one morning they plainly saw a mermaid, who played for a moment on the surface of the sea and then with a flourish of her fishy tail disappeared in the cold depths. Hudson's account of the mermaid is as follows:

The fifteenth, all day and night clear sunshine. The latitude at noon 75 degrees, seven minutes. We held westward by our account 13 leagues. In the afternoon the sea was assuaged and the wind being at east we set sail and stood south by east and south south-east as we could. This morning one of our company looking overboard saw a mermaid and calling up some of the company to see her one more came up, and by that time she was come close to the ship's side, looking earnestly on the men ; a little after the sea came and overturned her ; from the navil upwards her back and breasts were like a woman's, as they say that saw her ; her body was as big as one of us ; her skin very white, and long hair hanging down behind, of color black. In her going down they saw her tail which was like the tail of a porpoise and speckled like a mackerel. Their names that saw her were Thomas Hilles and Robert Raynor.

Hudson finally abandoned with great reluctance his cherished hope of passing to the north of Nova Zembla. Baffled by the persistent ice-fields he sorrowfully turned southward, to find if possible some other channel through which he might sail to the eastern side of the islands.

On the 26th of June, in fair sunshiny weather, he approached for the first time the land that he had been so long skirting, and sighted a point that he identified with the headland called by the Dutch navigators Swart Cliff, or Swarte Klip. Some of his commentators have believed this first landfall to be the South

Goose Cape.   When within two miles of this land he
sent his mate, Robert Juet, with the boatswain and
four of the men, ashore in the ship's boat to fill
several of the water-casks "and to see what the land
might yield that might be profitable."

The little exploring party found and brought aboard
a curious assortment of things that they had picked up
on the shore, whales' fins and deer horns being among
the number, and they reported fresh streams of water
beside which, in the low ground, the young grass of
that season pushed up between the dried blades of the
old grass "a shaftman long."   It was very hot on
shore, Hudson tells us, and the snow was melting
rapidly and running away in the streams.   The oozy
ground bore the footprints of many wild animals, deer,
bears, and foxes being particularly abundant.

"They went from us at three o'clock in the morning"—so runs the account—"and came aboard at a
south-east sunne."   It was the land and the season of
the unsetting sun.

> At their coming wee saw two or three com-
> panies of morses in the sea near us swimming,
> being almost calm.   I presently sent my mate,
> Ludlow the carpenter and six others a shore, to a
> place where I thought the morses might come on
> the shoare ; they found the place likely, but found
> no signe of any that had been there.   There was
> a crosse standing on the shoare, much driftwood,
> and signs of fires that had beene made there,
> They saw the footing of very great deere and
> beares, and much fowle, and a foxe ; they brought

aboord whale finnes, some mosse, flowers and greene things that did there grow. They brought also two pieces of a crosse, which they found there.   .   The sunnes height was 4 degrees, 45 minutes; inclination 22 degees 33 minutes, which makes the latitude 72 degrees, 12 minutes. There is a disagreement between this and the last observation; but by meanes of the cleerenesse of the sunne, the smoothenesse of the sea and the neernesse to land, we could not be deceived, and care was taken in it.

The next entry in the log evidently refers to the same anchorage.

The eighth and twentieth at four in the morning our boat came aboard and brought two dozen of fowls and some eggs, whereof a few were good.   .   In this calm from eight o'clock last evening 'till four this morning, we were drawn back to the northward as far as we were last evening at four o'clock, by a stream or tide, and we chose rather to drive than to adventure the loss of an anchor and the spoil of a cable. Here our new ship boat began to do us service and was an encouragement to my company, which want I found last year.

His reference to the new ship's boat would seem to indicate that the second voyage was made, like the first, in the staunch little *Hopewell*.

The prevalence of wild fowls noticed in a preceding paragraph is still characteristic of Nova Zembla, and caused that portion of the shore to be called the Goose Coast. The driftwood found by Hudson in quantities

on the coast of Nova Zembla is still a common feature
of that locality. This flotsam is carried thousands of
miles—not infrequently, Asher assures us, from the
American coast—by the Gulf Stream, and is deposited
upon the shores of islands within the arctic circle. It
is by such indications, in part, that the Gulf Stream
and its consequent current within the arctic circle has
been charted. Upon the morning of the 29th of June,
there being no wind, Hudson again ordered the boat
manned and the *Hopewell*, using both sails and oars,
was towed towards a point of land where it was
thought walrus herds might have gone ashore.
Rounding the point Hudson caused the anchor to be
dropped near an island in the mouth of a river.
There, the weather continuing calm and hot, they
rode till the next day, though twice obliged to shift
their anchorage by reason of the floating ice brought
down by the current of the river.

The 30th, Hudson's record, was

> calm, hot and faire weather; we weighed in the
> morning and towed and rowed, and at noone we
> came to anchor neere the ile aforesaid in the
> mouth of the river, and saw very much ice driv-
> ing in the sea, two leagues without us, lying
> south-east and north-west, and driving to the
> north-west so fast that wee coulde not by twelve
> a clocke at night see it out of the top. At the
> iland where we rode lieth a little rocke, whereon
> were fortie or fiftie morses lying asleep, being all
> that it could holde, it being so full and so little.
> I sent my companie ashoare to them, leaving none

aboord but my boy and me [the boy in this case was probably Hudson's own son, John]. By meanes of their neernesse to the water, they all got away, save one which they killed and brought his head aboord ; and ere they came aboord they went on the iland, which is reasonable high and steep. They killed and brought with them a great fowle, whereof there were many, and likewise some egges, and in an houre they came aboord. This ile is two flight-shot over in length, and one in bredth.

We may take up Henry Hudson's yard-stick to measure a distance : a flight-shot means a shot from a cross-bow, or possibly the flight of a shaft from a long bow, which would be between five hundred and a thousand feet. A long bow will carry five hundred feet and a cross-bow twice that distance.

At midnight our anchor came home and we tayled aground by meanes of the strength of the streame ; but by the help of God, we hoved her off without hurt. In short time we moved our ship, and rode still all night ; and in the night we had a little wind at east and east south-east. Wee had at noone this day an observation and were in the latitude of 71 degrees 15 minutes.

On the 1st of July the explorer lay in a calm a few leagues to the north of the point where the last observation was made. Here he records that he sent "my mate Everet" and four of the sailors ashore in a boat to discover whether any rivers emptied into the bay where he had found anchorage for his vessel, and also to note "where morses did come to land." The "mate Everet" is only our old acquaintance Juet masquerading under another name.   We are constantly reminded of the want of regularity in the spelling of personal names at the time of which we are writing.   Reference has been made to the almost endless variety to which Hudson's own name was orthographically subjected.   Juet, by the substitution of the equivalents I and v, for J and u, becomes Ivet and is so spelled by some historians.   Between Ivet and Everet the difference is too slight to have troubled a seventeenth century scribe.   There is not the slightest reason to suppose that Juet and Everet were other than identical.

Had there been a sportsman's magazine published in 1608 Hudson would have been a valued contributor. His journal abounds in descriptions of fish, flesh, and fowl—one hardly knows where to class such creatures as mermaids—and although he does not seem personally to have engaged actively in the chase, yet he encouraged his men upon every opportunity to pursue the walrus, lay in stores of wild fowl, and track the bear and deer.   Over the prevalence of whales, for the capture of which the *Hopewell* seems not to have been adequately equipped, he waxes enthusiastic, probably forseeing the potential importance of that noble quarry.

Hudson was keenly alive to the blow which his plans had received when the ice pack compelled him to turn southward.   "When by means of the great plenty of ice, the hope of passage between Newland

and Nova Zembla was taken away " he wrote, " My purpose was by the Vaygats to pass by the mouth of the river Ob, and to double that way the north cape of Tartaria or to give the reason whereof it will not be." Commenting upon this passage, Dr. Asher says:

> Hudson seemed to think that when he had once passed the north cape of Tartary (Cape Tabin?), the rest of the undertaking to reach China by a north-east route would be quite as easy and hardly worth mentioning. This was also Sebastian Cabot's idea and that of all his disciples down to our navigator. Ortelius' maps, the best expression of the geographical dogma of the age, imply a similar belief. The northern coast of Asia, which is there drawn almost from fancy, is everywhere too far south. The voyage from the *Promontorium Scythecum* to Cathay, or northern China, appears on these maps as quite an easy matter.

The previous explorations of Stephen Burrough and others confirmed the errors while adding to the knowledge of geographers.

Had Hudson known of the broader Kara Strait or even of Matthew Strait, it is probable that he would never have attempted the arduous voyage around the northern end of Nova Zembla. The river which he had entered in pursuit of the walrus herd now tempted him with the hope that it might prove a passage to the other side of the islands. He dispatched his mate Juet, with several of the crew, in

a boat to explore the river, which they did for
several leagues. They found the water deep and
salt as that of the ocean, and the width of the
stream they reported to be six or eight miles. At
twenty fathoms they found no bottom. Here also
the wild fowl, foxes, deer, and walrus were plentiful.
Juet's report greatly encouraged Hudson, and his
hope, that certainly sprang perennial, was raised to
expectation once more. He was sure that this
sound would take him whither he wanted to go;
and therefore he set sail to explore it, ascending for
nine or ten leagues, when as the wind failed him
he anchored and again sent the mate with five men
to explore. Juet and his companions were absent
on this expedition until the next day, when they
returned almost exhausted with labour and exposure. Their report was disappointing; they had
found shoal water at a distance of twenty miles beyond the vessel, the depth being not more than
four feet.

Foiled in this attempt to reach the sea he sought,
the navigator went, as he says, "with sorrow that
our labour was vain, for had this sound held as it
did make good show of, for depth, breadth, safeness
of harbour, and good anchor ground, it might have
yielded an excellent passage to the more easterly
sea."

The summer was passing. Again Hudson had
been obliged to yield to the forces of nature, and
his second expedition, like the first, had ended in

failure. There was nothing left for him but to return to England. He resolved before commencing the homeward voyage to visit the land which the English claimed to have been discovered by Sir Hugh Willoughby. His idea seemed to have been mainly to follow the herds of walrus or morse that had been driven from Nova Zembla by the ice.

Willoughby land has been one of the disputed points of Arctic geography. Whether the Dutch maps that place that land to the south-east of Spitzbergen were correct, as the journal of Willoughby and the description of several geographers of that day seems to prove, or whether the land in question was really only a part of Spitzbergen, is difficult to decide. Hudson believed it to be a distinct island or group. The whole history of maritime exploration is punctuated with islands which now appear upon no chart. These evanescent islands were not always imaginary; we have abundant evidence that in every ocean there have been some that have appeared and disappeared like the figments of a dream. One such island at least appeared upon the coast of Iceland not more than a century ago, remained above the waves long enough to be named and then sank again to the bed of the ocean from which it had been impelled by some volcanic impulse. The same thing has happened in the harbour of Rhodes and in the broad waters of the Pacific. Ten or twelve years ago a gentleman in the consular service of the United States reported a newly

risen islet almost in the track of the mail steamers
to the Far East, and since this chapter was commenced another has been reported by an American
war vessel off the north-western coast of the United
States. Whoever will follow the transcript made by
Las Casas of the journal kept by Columbus, and
will try to square his description of San Salvador
and the islands adjacent to it with any modern ad-
miralty or hydrographic office chart, must be convinced that no island such as the first of those
discovered by the great Genoese exists above water
to-day. There are numberless instances of islands
that have come and gone, from the time of Atlantis, to which Plato testified, to the latest born
Pacific atoll. Enough has been said on this subject to show that it is not impossible that Wil-
loughbyland, which the Dutch geographers described
and which our English mariner sought, may have
been a real island and no myth, although the explorer of to-day may fail to find it.

Hudson was unsuccessful in his search for Willough-
byland. The first point he sighted, after sailing westward for many leagues, was Wardhus, in Lapland.
Soon afterwards he rounded the North Cape and stood
away for home. Dropping down the Norway coast
towards the end of July, he noted that the nights
became dark, so that for the first time in many weeks
he was obliged to place a lamp in the binnacle. Once,
before finally reaching England, he hesitated, being
filled with a wish to turn towards Greenland, the

coasts of which seemed always to possess for him a peculiar fascination. Guided however by his better judgment he hastened southward and arrived in the Thames on the 26th day of August, after a four months' voyage.

Hudson's employers were evidently discouraged by his second failure and offered him no immediate opportunity to retrieve his reputation or indulge his passion for exploration. His fame, nevertheless, had by this time spread abroad, so that flattering overtures were made to him by both French and Dutch companies. He has been sharply criticised for accepting finally the propositions made by the Dutch East India company, but this objection seems to be fine drawn, as at the time his services were not desired by his own countrymen.

Under date of August 7, 1608, Hudson makes this curious note in the log :

> I used all diligence to arrive at London, and therefore now I gave my company a certificate under my hand, of my free and willing return without persuasion or force of any one of them ; for at my being at Nova Zembla the sixth of July and void of hope of a north-east passage except by the Waygates, which I was not fitted to try or prove, I therefore, resolved to use all means I could to sail to the north-west ; considering the time and means we had, if the wind should friend us as in the first part of our voyage it had done, and to make trial of that place called Lumley's inlet and the furious over fall of Captain Davis,

hoping to run into it an 100 leagues and to return
as God should enable me ; but now having spent
more than half the time I had and had gone but
the shortest part of the way, by means of contrary
winds, I thought it my duty to save victuals,
wages, and tackle, by my speedy return, and
not by foolish rashness, the time being wasted, to
lay more charge upon the action than necessity
should compel. I arrived at Gravesend the sixth
and twentieth of August.

CHAPTER IV

HE year 1609 was one of the notable range marks of history. It was a time of great events, of pivotal experiences. It was the year of the great truce, that promised a breathing space after thirty years of conflict between the Catholic powers and the Protestant Netherlands. It was the prelude to a more prolonged and decisive conflict. In 1609 Spain agreed to treat with the Netherlands "as with an independent power." Holland had fought for and had won her standing among the nations of Europe. In this very year her ambassadors were for the first time received at foreign courts upon an equality with the representatives of kings and emperors. They who had formerly been obliged to cool their heels in the anterooms of ministers, now treated proudly with sovereigns. The whole civilised world had been turned topsy turvy, and the States General of Holland, with France at their side, were upon the upper hemisphere.

Never was a revolution more far-reaching in its effects. The Holy Roman Empire was trembling;

Spain was exhausted; France was affectionate in
her regard to her republican ally, and England
was almost civil. It is true that the loosely constructed confederation known as the United Netherlands, was from its birth infected with the germs of an
internal disorder which before many years would prove
more menacing to its health and indeed to its very
existence than the animosity of all its enemies, but for
a time, before she was torn by religious and political
dissentions between her leading statesmen, theologians, and soldiers, she presented to the world an
almost invincible front.

Barneveld, the great advocate of the States General,
was the silent but mighty power that governed the republic. Henry IV., on the throne of France, with
Sully and Villeroy and a host of lesser councillors
about him, was the friend of Barneveld and the States.
Upon the Spanish throne was the boyish and inef-
ficient Philip, the slave and tool of his ministers.
Germany was an ant-hill of petty sovereigns acknow-
ledging the overlordship of the Holy Roman Empire.
Italy was hardly more than a name; Austria was mis-
governed and disorganised; James of Scotland and
England, "the most learned fool in Christendom," sat
upon the throne that Elizabeth had made secure, and
which Cromwell was to make great, but which under
his weak rule could hardly be rated as of the first-class.
In what is now Russia, the Duke of Muscovy had
made a beginning and had indeed assumed the title
of Tzar, but Russia as we know it did not exist; the

Sultan of Turkey, the Dey of Algiers, even the electors of petty European principalities, were more influential in the world's politics.

There was no America—a wilderness to be explored lay between the provinces of New France, Virginia, and the Spanish possessions.

The Hanseatic League dominated trade in Germany, as the East India company did in the low countries and as the Muscovy company and the mercantile corporations did in England. Even these great organisations were touched with the prevailing impulse to war, and sent armed expeditions to extort by piratical means what they could not wrest from their rivals in trade. Nor were their armaments without excuse. At that time the high seas were laid under tribute by pirates, of whom Simon Danzig was a fair example. This man, a Zeelander by birth, had been in the employ of the Netherlands till it suited him to exercise upon his own account the trade of war that he had learned from his employers. On his own responsibility he raised and commanded a fleet of pirates that in turn terrorised the merchant convoys of Spain, France, Portugal, England, and Holland. Danzig made most of the rulers of Europe pay tribute or blackmail as the price of immunity from his marauders. His name recalls Longfellow's verse:

> " Simon Danz has come home again
> From cruising about with his buccaneers ;
> He has singed the beard of the King of Spain,
> And carried away the dean of Gean,
> And sold him in Algiers,"

This stanza contains nothing that needs to be explained or excused on the score of poetic licence, except perhaps the use of the word buccaneer. The account of Danzig's exploits as here given, is approximately accurate. Danzig was only one of many pirates that added unwelcome zest to seafaring life three centuries ago. He was the type of a class that carried out on the high seas the same lawless spirit that dominated the cities no less than the fields and forests of Europe. If asked to characterise the age in which Henry Hudson lived, one must point to its evidences of unbridled brutality and greed run mad. The lust for power, fame, fortune; the aggrandisement of the ruler, the enrichment of the merchant, the lawlessness of the soldier made a world with little in it of peace or comfort for the ordinary man, the world's plodder, the sober, sombre worker in the hive, whose industry affords a prey to innumerable marauders.

It was an age when no man's fortune, no woman's honour was safe in any part of the known world. In no country of Christendom was the law strong enough to protect its citizens from rapine and outrage. To travel from town to town meant to take one's life in hand, and whether on sea or land the adventurous voyager armed himself cap-a-pie and trusted to chance and his own prowess to reach the end of his journey.

Let those who decry present conditions and doubt the world's advance look narrowly and thoughtfully at the disadvantages under which life at its best was lived three short centuries ago.

The Danzigs afloat and ashore furnished the excuse for warlike accessories to mercantile ventures. The fleets of those who traded in silks and spices, in furs and food-stuffs, went armed with culverins and demi-culverins, carronades and falconets, ready to fight their way through not only stormy seas, but opposing pirates, to reach their proposed market.

The great Dutch explorers and navigators were, unless history belies them, notorious freebooters. Even Henry Hudson, voyaging towards America in the *Half Moon*, seeing a strange sail pursued it till nightfall, with what purpose we are not informed. In estimating the character of men of the sixteenth and seventeenth centuries, let us be careful not to measure them by twentieth century standards. They will almost invariably fall short.

The leading centres of commerce in the sixteenth century, as we have already noticed, were Burghes, Ghent, and Antwerp. Those great hives of industry with their precious stores of merchandise and accumulated capital were the special objects of Spanish attack during those years of horror in which Duke Alva gained for himself the title by which he will always be best known,— ' the Scourge of the Netherlands.'' The pillage of these cities by the combined armies of Spain and Germany rendered destitute at least three hundred thousand families, who fled from their own land to find asylums in other countries.

The larger proportion of the most energetic and resourceful of the Flemish merchants made their home in Holland, particularly in Amsterdam, and to that influx of brains and skill was due much of the commercial supremacy that made the States General for a time one of the most powerful governments in Christendom.

These great merchants at the time when Henry Hudson stood before them, were arriving at a pinnacle of power and state such as no merchants save those of Venice had ever before attained. They were indeed the princes of trade, before whom all men except the most exalted, doffed the cap. Van Rensselaer, the pearl merchant of Amsterdam, afterwards the most powerful patroon of the upper Hudson, was a type of the class to which belonged Usselincx, de Vrees, Moucheron, Mahu, Godyn, and l'Heremite. The strong organisation which included many of these powerful men had a closer relation with the state and the policy of statesmen than may be imagined. Olden Barneveld, who in 1669 was still actually, though not nominally, the political head of the Netherland Confederation, was the great exponent of so-called republican, or Arminian, principles, and it was his care that the control of the East India company should be in the hands of those who shared his political faith. Second only to Barneveld in power and influence was his friend, the young juror, Hugo de Groot, or Grotius.

Who that has read the wonderful story of the great struggle between the Protestant Netherlands and the great Catholic powers can forget Grotius, the friend of the advocate Barneveld, the philosopher, historian, and jurist, whom Henry IV. admired and Maurice of Orange feared? When Hudson made his agreement with the East India company Grotius had put ten years of splendid effort after his maiden case at the bar of the Hague. His *Mare Liberum*, in which he defended the freedom of the Dutch East India trade, was a document of incalculable importance to the merchants of the Netherlands. Ten years later he would share in the trial and condemnation of Barneveld, though not in that great statesman's execution. In the year of which I am writing Grotius was Fiscal General, a strong supporter of the "Remonstrants" and a prominent figure in the political life of the Netherlands. It must not be forgotten that his chief work, *De Jure Belli et Pacis* has been translated into many tongues and is to-day familiar to students of international law, as the basis of that science.

CHAPTER V

UDSON found in 1609 no immediate chance of employment by his own countrymen. His two voyages in 1607 and 1608 had won him celebrity, but their success was not great enough to warrant the Muscovy Company in undertaking immediate plans for a new venture along the same lines. It is probable that while the general public understood vaguely that the *Hopewell* had gone far into the frozen Northern sea and had visited strange lands, yet that public had never understood the purpose of the voyages nor measured their failure. The Muscovy Company worked as far as possible under conditions of secrecy and it did not publish its plans nor confide to the world the details of its discoveries ; indeed the only chart known to have found its way to the light from its secret archives is said to have been stolen by one of its captains, who left England because of debt and took the map with him. We may suppose that the company, though loath to repeat an unsuccessful experiment, kept its disappointment locked up with its other secrets, and that the world at large, while recognising the gallant effort and stirred by the romantic adventures of Hudson, was entirely blind to the fact that he had not succeeded in the main object of his enterprise.

The navigator's fame soon reached Holland, where, though the zeal for arctic exploration had languished since the last unsuccessful efforts of Heemskirk and Barentz, yet the merchants were always alive to an opportunity to maintain their commercial supremacy. We cannot lay too great stress upon the probability that the news of Hudson's voyages came to the merchants of Amsterdam as the story of a great success. Already jealous of the increasing rivalry of the English traders, those of Holland saw in the achievement of Henry Hudson an added menace to their own interests. The very secrecy which the Muscovy Company maintained made the danger seem all the greater.

In August, 1603, six years before Hudson's visit to Holland, the committee of control of the Dutch East India Company passed a formal resolution to prevent by every means in its power the ascendency of its English rivals. What wonder then that the response of the Amsterdam governors of that company to the reports of Hudson's northern voyages was an invitation to the Englishman to visit Holland and discuss the terms of an expedition in their service.

In the winter following his second voyage Hudson left London to comply with the request of the Dutch

Company. Let us frankly admit that he has been severely criticised for a step which some writers have held to be disloyal to his own country. We may conjecture that the aspect of the case which would have appealed most strongly to a merchant, that is, the question of international trade rivalry, would seem to a sailor of slight importance. In deciding upon a change of masters, no doubt the purely personal question of employment was an important factor. We have no reason to suppose that Hudson could afford to remain inactive, and since the Muscovy Company were not prepared to risk a third expedition where two had already produced nothing, he no doubt felt justified, and was justified, in making terms with new employers. The employment of Englishmen by either the merchants or the government of Holland was not unusual. John Romeyn Broadhead, while engaged in his admirable researches at The Hague, discovered and copied a letter written in 1614 [the year of the formation of the West India Company] to the States General of Holland from King James I. of England, in which occur these words:

> We cannot but acknowledge the favour, which through regard for Us you have done to Sir Thomas Dale, Marshal of Virginia, by permitting him to be absent for some time from your service, to which he should already have returned, had not all of the colony where he has right worthily comported himself, perceiving the necessity of his remaining among them to settle and give stability to that enterprise, supplicated Us to interpose

again with you and to request you to permit his absence two or three years more, in order that he may complete the work so well begun.

The king's letter to the States was duly answered and the request granted, a resolution to that effect passing the chamber on Tuesday, the last day of September, 1614.

> Received and read a letter from the king of Great Britain, dated at Leicester, the 19th of August, old style, in favour of Captain Sir Thomas Dale, Marshal of Virginia, to the effect that their High Mightinesses would please give leave of absence to the same captain for two or three years more.   .   After deliberation . . . their High Mightinesses have agreed and consented thereto.

There is a homely old adage to the effect that "compliments fly when quality meets." King James petitioning his neighbours the States General for a continued leave of absence for an Englishman in their service, is an edifying bit of politeness from one who claimed the revenues of certain Hollandish ports to liquidate an old debt, and had at times maintained English soldiers there to enforce the claim, and who, not more than three or four years before, had suggested to the Dutch ambassadors in London that he could not treat with them as with an equal power because of seigneurial rights over them. That the alleged overlordship existed only in the king's somewhat unbalanced imagination, did not make it easier to sustain diplomatic relations between the two countries. The jealousy which seems to have sprung up between the subjects of James and the countrymen of Maurice had its origin in something more bitter than trade rivalry. Gen. John Meredith Read, Jr., in an address delivered forty years ago, says:

> It is probable that Van Meteren, the Dutch Consul resident in London, was employed to conduct the negotiations (of the Dutch East India Company) with Hudson. The arguments of this learned man were calculated to have great weight with one whose whole energies were devoted to extending the range of geographical knowledge. The Historian may have convinced Hudson that under new auspices he would possess larger opportunities for accomplishing the wish of his life. . . . Our acquaintance with his character and our knowledge of his purpose and plans must convince us that it was the desire to crown the labours of his life with the triumphant discovery of a northern passage to India, which controlled Hudson's action in this matter.

The negotiations suggested by the Amsterdam directors of the Dutch Company were commenced at once upon Hudson's arrival in Holland. The preliminary discussions as to the possibility and advisability of the northern route to China probably did not consume much time, since they touched upon articles of a common faith. Hudson's belief was, as already shown, an inheritance from Cabot, Davis, and Frobisher; the result of a life-long training. The directors were steeped in the theories of Barentz and Heemskirk. It was a notable gathering of

merchants, who were indeed the princes of their
guild, that confronted the English mariner and
listened with close attention to his exposition of
his theories and plans. They were men who were
accustomed to conduct great affairs. Not all, perhaps not a majority, of the Amsterdam chamber,
were Hollanders by birth. Grave political changes
had made Amsterdam the asylum for the great
captains of industry from all the Low Countries.
The assembly that Hudson faced was probably
second to no mercantile association that has ever
met for the consideration of an important trade
question.

Among these Lords of Trade sat one of the most
notable geographers of the day, the learned and
Reverend Peter Plantius, who proved an ally of Hudson from the beginning of the conference until its
close. It is possible that their acquaintance may have
commenced at an earlier date in London, as their intercourse suggests more than a passing acquaintance.
The scholarly Plantius was a minister of the Reformed
Church, Flemish by birth, and a traveller even in his
youth. His education was obtained in his own country,
in England, and in Germany ; in 1577 he was ordained
to the ministry, and for six years officiated in the Reformed Church in Brussels, from which he was trans-
ferred when the city was taken by the Duke of Parma.
Doffing his clerical gown, he put on the uniform of a
soldier, and in that disguise escaped to Holland.   He
was set over a church in Amsterdam, was a member of

the synod of Dort in 1618, and was one of the committee of scholars who translated the Old Testament into the Dutch language. To this man Holland owed much of her enthusiasm for navigation and discovery. He is reputed to have been the founder of a school of navigation in the city of his adoption, and became famous, not only in his own but also in foreign lands, as one of the foremost geographical scholars of the age. Plantius is said to have been interested in a financial way in a subsequent expedition to the Hudson River. His death occurred in Amsterdam in 1622, when he had reached the age of seventy years.

When the navigator began to explain his belief in an open polar sea, giving in support of that theory cogent arguments drawn from his own observation and experience, Plantius brought the weight of his geographical knowledge and reputation to the Englishman's support. Hudson made a favourable impression upon the Amsterdam directors, though among them were a few who questioned the wisdom of sending good money after bad, recalling the failures of some notable Dutch navigators to discover a passage through the ice-bound northern sea. Foremost among those who opposed the project was a prominent merchant, Balthazar Moucheron, who had himself financed at least one arctic voyage, and had become convinced that there was nothing to be gained by another. His objection was opposed by the influence of Plantius.

Among the Belgian contingent in Amsterdam no man stood higher than Balthazar de Moucheron, who indeed has been called "the father of Dutch commerce." He was a pioneer, sending vessels into strange seas, into the unknown north and the distant orient. His fleets were among the first to explore the Arctic Ocean and the waters of Northern Russia. His captains penetrated every distant sea. This de Moucheron's opposition to Henry Hudson's proposed voyage was decided and sane. Lambrechtsen Van Ritthem, in his history of New Netherland, says:

> The inclination of the directors of the East India Company were much at variance with the proposals of Hudson. The directors of Zealand opposed it; they were probably discouraged by the fruitless results of former voyages, concerning which they could obtain sufficient information from their colleague, Balthazar Moucheron, who long before had traded with the north. If private merchants would run the risk they had no objection, provided the Company was not injured by it. The Amsterdam directors nevertheless would not give up their plan and sent Henry Hudson in the same year, 1609, with a yacht called the *Half Moon*, manned by sixteen Englishmen and Hollanders.

Jodicus Hondius, the second friend to whose influence Hudson was greatly indebted, acted as his interpreter with the directors of the East India Company, and signed the contract as witness. He was held in great esteem in Amsterdam as an engraver of maps and a man of considerable geographical knowledge. Like Plantius, Hondius was a native of Flanders and had also been for some years a resident of London. There he won recognition as an engraver, being employed upon portraits of the Queen, Drake, Cavendish, and others.

The objections raised by Moucheron's party to the employment of the English navigator at least had the effect of tempering the zeal of those who had invited him to come to Holland, so that they began to find unforeseen objections to the immediate carrying out of their plans. In the first place, it was pointed out, the matter should be taken up by the whole body of the East India Company and not by the Amsterdam chamber alone. There were the Zealand and other chambers that were entitled to be heard and to have a share in the enterprise. Unfortunately the next regular meeting of the committee which constituted the governing body of the company would not be held for several months, and it would then be too late to undertake a voyage to the north during that year.

It was finally decided that Hudson should be reimbursed for his expenses in visiting Holland, and a provisional promise made to employ him in 1610, the proviso being that the committee of governors approved the project.

So the negotiation with the East India Company was interrupted in what must have been a very unsatisfactory way for a sailor whose bread and butter depended upon his employment. He had dreamed great dreams and the Amsterdam merchants treated him kindly and told him to wait a year for their final

answer. Hudson, however, did not immediately leave
Amsterdam, whatever may have been his intention
when dismissed by the merchants. Among the
acquaintances that he had formed was one with a
merchant named Isaac Le Maire, at one time a member
of the Amsterdam Chamber of the East India Company. I do not know whether Le Maire's connection
with that body was severed before or after Hudson's
visit, nor whether it terminated under compulsion or
by his own wish. It is not possible to say what his
relations to the company were in the early part of
1609; but there is good evidence that almost immediately after the close of the conference with the
merchants Le Maire approached Hudson with a
scheme and a proposition, which, if successfully
carried out, would have put our navigator in the employ of that most powerful of kings, Henry IV. of
France.

Hudson seems to have talked of his theories, hopes,
and plans with all a sailor's proverbial frankness. He
recounted to Le Maire his adventures, and no doubt
expressed his disappointment at the treatment
accorded him by the East India Company's local representatives. Whether Le Maire was moved to enthusiasm by Hudson's narration, or was animated by
animosity to the Dutch East India Company, or simply
and selfishly planned for his own financial good, he
carried the whole story at once to Pierre Jeannin,
Henry's representative at The Hague, and one of
the king's most trusted councillors.

President Jeannin, who subsequently succeeded the great Sully as Minister of Finance in France, had been previously employed as ambassador to England, where he may possibly have become acquainted with Hudson, who doubtless was known to him by reputation. It was a fortunate occurrence that again brought Hudson prominently before Jeannin, fixing the minister's attention upon the navigator and his work, for it is to Jeannin that we owe our knowledge of several facts not elsewhere recorded that relate to Hudson and his voyages. Le Maire's visits to the Frenchman were made secretly. His introduction of Hudson chimed well with a plan that was dear to the heart of the French king.

While the relations of Henry with the States General of Holland were not only friendly but intimate, and his opinion of Barneveld, the powerful advocate of the States General, higher than that accorded by him to any other statesman in Europe, yet these facts did not prevent his feeling a strong jealousy of the trade ascendency won by the Dutch, and cherishing a secret purpose to rob them of it. It did not matter that Henry stood behind the States General in their extended and troublesome peace negotiations with Spain, and that he frequently reminded their representative at his court that he was their patron and protector. The greatest source of their wealth he coveted, as he did most things—as he made war or love—with all his soul.

So indissolubly were the affairs of the merchants and

the politics of states bound together in those troubled days, that some knowledge of both is necessary to a clear understanding of either. Francis Aerssens, the diplomatic representative of the States in Paris, one of the cleverest diplomats and politicians of his time, noted with great concern that Isaac Le Maire and other prominent Dutch lords of trade were secretly at the house of the king's intimate councillor, Zamet, in Paris. He reported to his chief, Barneveld, that Le Maire was having daily conferences with the king. This matter, implying as it must have done, treachery on the part of Le Maire towards the mercantile interests of Holland, gave great concern to Barneveld and his colleagues. Unfortunately we have no means of knowing what part the Advocate's knowledge of this intrigue played in terminating Le Maire's membership in the Dutch East India Company.

Le Maire's interviews with Henry, as well as his correspondence with Hudson and Jeannin, were with a view to the formation of a French East India Company, which should, under royal patronage, deflect at least a portion of the lucrative oriental trade that was enriching the Netherlands.

Through the information furnished by Aerssens the Advocate was able to baffle the plots of his royal friend and the machinations of Le Maire. It was perhaps due to his authority and influence—though we may merely conjecture, having no documentary authority to support such a view—that the Amsterdam Chamber resumed its negotiations with Hudson. There can be little doubt that both the hero of Ivry and the powerful Advocate of the States General were factors in the life of Henry Hudson, and indirectly responsible for his voyage in 1609.

The full text of Jeannin's letter to Henry IV. at the time of Le Maire's presentation of Hudson is too important to be altogether omitted and the reader will find it in a subsequent chapter.

However the news of Hudson's interviews with Le Maire and Jeannin reached the ears of the merchants, or under whatever influence, they recalled the sailor at once, and with a decision and energy greatly in contrast with their former dilatory proceedings made a formal contract with him, having found a simple way to overcome the obstacle that but a short time before they had supposed to be insurmountable. The Committee of Seventeen was composed of members of the boards of directors in several principal cities. The Amsterdam board, having concluded and completed its contract with Hudson, sent copies of the document to their colleagues in other cities for their signatures. It was clearly a case in which red tape must be sacrificed to an unyielding emergency. There were, to be sure, protests from the New Zealand directors, but these were overruled, and preparations were forthwith made for the important voyage.

There are several points worth noting in the contract drawn up by the company and signed by its officers and by Hudson on the 8th of January, 1609. The first thing that attracts our attention is that the navigator is styled in that instrument Henry Hudson and not Hendrik. Here disappears the last possible excuse for calling the English explorer of the North River of New Netherland by any other than his English baptismal name. Hudson's negotiations with the Company and the completion of his agreement with it, required the services of an interpreter, which is evidence that he did not understand the Dutch language thoroughly, if at all.

The company's representatives agreed to furnish a little vessel of about sixty tons, to provision and man her before the first day of April, by which time Hudson was to sail "by the north around the north side of Nova Zembla." The instructions were clear and unequivocal upon this point, that the navigator was not to think of attempting any other route than that set down, and failing to accomplish that was to return to Holland, where the subject of another voyage might be discussed. The payment agreed upon for his services was one which we would consider ridiculously small, and which even at that time was not commensurate either with the fame of the sailor or the magnitude of his undertaking. He was to be paid the equivalent of $320.00 for his personal outfit and for the support of his wife and children, and in case he lost his life his widow was to receive $80.00 in addition to this sum. This item is doubly interesting because we find in it proof that Hudson had a wife and one or more children besides John, who was the young companion of several of his voyages. It is the only evi-

dence that we have on this point.   The master was
to be further rewarded at the discretion of his employers if he found the desired passage.

The *Half Moon* was fitted out according to the agreement, and was manned by a mixed crew of Englishmen
and Hollanders, probably not more than sixteen in all.
We know that some members of this crew had sailed
with Hudson on one or more of his previous voyages.
Robert Juet notably, and John Hudson possibly, accompanied the navigator as before. Coleman, whose
name is familiar as one of those who had followed
Hudson's fortunes for two years, shipped for this
voyage also, though he did not return from it. We
may suppose that Hudson felt keenly the death of this
man, after whom Coleman's Point, at the entrance to
New York Harbor, was named. He had been a faithful and trusted member of the ship's company aboard
the little *Hopewell*, and had shared with the master
the perils and hardships of his Arctic voyages.

We have no means of ascertaining what proportion
of the crew of the *Half Moon* were Dutch, nor can we
tell, except by their subsequent conduct, what the
character of the Hollanders may have been. The
majority, there seems reason to believe, were previously
employed in East Indian or other southern waters, and
were not sufficiently inured to cold to make them de-
sirable sailors for an Arctic voyage.

Something should be said of the vessel in which
Henry Hudson was to make one of the most important
voyages that history records. The *Half Moon*, or as

the Dutch authors sometimes spelled it, " *Halve Maene*," was what was called a Vlie boat. The name comes from the island of Vlie, or Vlieland, lying to the north of Texel, at the entrance to the Zuyder Zee. The small trading or fishing boats that plied over the shoals of the Vlieland passage were built with almost flat bottoms. From them is descended the English flyboat.

The *Half Moon* was a Vlie boat of eighty lasts burden. The last, like the ton, has been a somewhat flexible measure, but it is safe to say that the vessel in which Hudson sailed in 1609 was a shallow little craft of not over a hundred and sixty tons, and probably less. That she escaped the dangers of unknown and stormy seas and accomplished a journey extending from the Arctic circle to the shoals of the upper Hudson is to be counted one of the marvels of maritime history.

In a Dutch document which may be supposed to have some historical authority, mention is made of the " *Good Hope*" as having been fitted for Hudson's use in 1609. This may have been a slip of the pen or a copyist's error, or possibly Hudson commenced his voyage with more than one vessel. Whatever the fact may have been it is certain that in the main part of the voyage the *Half Moon* was unaccompanied by any other vessel.

CHAPTER VI

N the 4th of April, 1609, [new style] Henry Hudson cast loose from his moorings at Amsterdam and prepared to face the ice and battle with the fogs that had twice vanquished him. Two days later he passed the island of Texel and stood northward. His instructions were explicit; to go to the north of Nova Zembla and thence find his way by a southerly course till he should have reached the latitude of sixty degrees; or, in other words, till he should have come again as far south in the Eastern ocean as the parallel of the Shetland Islands, and thus beyond all possible menace from obstructing ice.

The course pursued after leaving the Zuyder Zee was practically that followed by Hudson in his voyage of the previous year. He was a month in reaching the North Cape, up to which time he had met with no striking adventures; but long before he could gain the coast of Nova Zembla he found himself in the grip of his old enemies, fog and ice. Another unfavourable influence was added to the forces of nature in combating the purpose of the explorer. His crew, enervated by warm latitudes, no sooner felt the rigorous arctic winds and the sickening chill of the enveloping fog, than they became mutinous.

Juet says nothing of a revolt in which it is not impossible that he bore a share, as he did upon a subsequent and more tragic occasion. His account of the earlier part of the voyage is by no means full or clear and his silence is in itself suggestive of concealment. Van Meteren, on the other hand, refers unequivocally to the mutiny of the crew ; and Van Meteren's account we suppose to have been drawn from conversations he had with Hudson, as well as from the navigator's written log of the voyage.

Knowing as we do that the Master of the *Half Moon* found it necessary to have an interpreter in his conferences with the Amsterdam merchants, we may infer that he could only direct the majority of his people through the mouth of his Dutch mate. So handicapped it would have been strange indeed if his control over them had been perfect. What stand was taken by the mate is unknown, but it is not improbable that he was the mouth-piece of the disaffected men.

After a fortnight of contrary winds, with dissensions among the crew that made the prosecution of the voyage impossible, Hudson was obliged to yield to the clamour of the forecastle. The vessel was turned about and the hope of a passage to the north of Nova Zembla abandoned, even before that land had been sighted.

The fact that Hudson reversed his plan and voyage under such irresistible pressure must, in the opinion of fair-minded critics, relieve him from censure. In this connection we may recall his remarkable and apparently gratuitous statement at the close of an earlier voyage, that he had not acted on compulsion when he turned back. The very fact that such a statement was thought necessary affords matter for reflection.

When the *Half Moon* headed westerly the North Cape was soon again in sight, the winds were favourable, the ice disappeared, the fog vanished. Down the western coast of Norway the little vessel sailed and her master faced in bitter anticipation the disappointment of his friends and the triumph of his enemies. With his return to Holland before midsummer, beaten ere his voyage was fairly begun, he knew that his reputation as a mariner would be irredeemably ruined and his hope of future employment in Holland wrecked. He had exhausted all the resources of his optimism in presenting his arguments to the merchants, and now he was returning to confess that he was not the man to carry out the plans that he had urged. That it was impossible to carry out those plans could only be admitted by confessing that his arguments had been without sufficient foundation. Never was navigator confronted by the horns of a more serious dilemma. Whichever way he chose, he must accept with it a stigma that would mean ruin to his ambition and even to his hope of livelihood. He was constantly drawing nearer to his starting point, nearer to the inevitable censure and disgrace that would attend the publication of his failure.

On the 22nd of April, according to Juet, "At ten of the clock we were thwart off Zenam.   .   The three and twentieth we steered along the land south-west and by west, eight leagues a watch .   .   and the distance is fifty leagues from the body of Zenam to the westernmost part of Lofoote.'' Zenam was probably Senjen Island, near the Norway coast, and by Lofoote is meant the Luffoden Islands, the westernmost being Vaero.

> On the twenty-sixth [runs the journal], was a great storm at the north-north-east and north-east. We steered away south-west, afore the wind, with our fore course abroad, for we were able to maintain no more sails, it blew so vehemently and the sea went so high and brake withall that it would have endangered a small ship to lie under the sea, so we scudded seventy leagues in four and twenty hours.

With the abatement of the tempest and the engrossing responsibility and labour it entailed, the navigator had time again to think of that great serious body, the Amsterdam Chamber of the East India Company, before which he would so soon be stammering his excuses. The whole question required further time for thought. In the meanwhile the water casks needed replenishing, and that duty afforded a reasonable excuse for a westerly course as far as the Faroe Islands, to the north of which he had passed on his first voyage. To that strange group he therefore set his course, from about the latitude of sixty-eight degrees.

Among what we may believe to be Hudson's valid claims as an original discoverer, is one recorded in Juet's journal of the third voyage. When twenty-five days out from Amsterdam, "we made our way west by north till noon. *Then we observed the sun having a slake.*" According to Dr. Asher the word slake, as a substantive, is a north country word meaning—according to Broket—"an accumulation of mud or slime, from slijak, etc." If, as this etymology indicates, Hudson observed a sun spot on the 21st of March, 1609, he was the earliest discoverer who has recorded this most interesting phenomenon. The observation of Thomas Hariot, which is generally considered the first of its kind on record, was made more than a year and a half later than that of Hudson. The Master of the *Half Moon* had the disadvantage of working without a telescope.

The Faroe Islands, surrounded by rocky barriers and dangerous whirlpools, are like those dragon-guarded islands of fable upon which, when the circle of enchantment was passed, the invader found pleasant gardens and balmy airs. They are to-day probably little changed from what they were in Hudson's time. Their inhabitants, cut off for centuries from the rest of the world, speak what is supposed to be the only living *patois* of the ancient Norse tongue. The air of the islands is mild the year round, so that even in winter cattle and sheep are herded without shelter, and snow so seldom lies upon the ground that the grazing is practically uninterrupted. To this curiously guarded, curiously favoured group Hudson sailed for his water supply, and the grumblers of his crew were apparently content to listen to the captain's propositions.

At four o'clock in the afternoon of the 28th of May the lookout on board the *Half Moon* saw in the distance the lofty crags of "the iles called Farre." Juet complains that they found them to lie fourteen leagues further east than the sea charts had indicated "for in running south-west from Lofoote wee had a good care to our steerage and observations; and counted ourselves thirty leagues off by our course and observation, and had sight of them sixteen or eighteen leagues off."

On the morning of the 29th it was what Juet calls fair weather, or as he explains, "sometimes calm and sometimes a gale," with the wind variable and the treacherous rocks of the shore menacing the vessel. Hudson at first looked in vain for a chance to enter some harbour. The dangerous volume of the ebb poured through the rocky channels as through so many sluiceways; so he coasted along the shores of the islands, standing away at nightfall and returning the following day, when he was fortunate enough to discover a passage between Strombo and Muggenes. Riding with the flood he entered a good harbour about nine o'clock in the morning; where, says the journal, "we went ashore to romage and filled all our empty casks with fresh water." It was evening when the

water was finally aboard and the "romaging" came
to an end.   We read that Hudson went ashore in the
morning to walk and was accompanied by most of his
crew; it appears probable that while in Strombo the
navigator came to an understanding with his men,
or at least that a conference was held there, for
immediately upon returning aboard they set sail.

Here we may believe that the Master of the *Half
Moon* finally decided upon a plan by which to escape
from his dilemma; a plan which involved disregard of
his sailing orders, but is held to have been justified by
the events that followed.   Even in making a decision
we find him pitiably handicapped.   He was, we believe, unable to go where he would unless he could
gain the permission of the mate and crew, whose con-
tumacy had already thwarted his dearest ambition.
Having asked for and gained their consent, he sailed
to the westward, first running south-west for the purpose of seeking Buss Island, one of Sir Martin Frobisher's supposed discoveries.   Unable to verify the
position of this land upon the chart, Hudson steered
the course proposed and for nearly a month encountered a succession of gales, in which he had
the misfortune to lose his foremast and otherwise
damage the *Half Moon*.

His plan, to carry out which he had found it necessary to obtain the consent of the crew, was to proceed
westerly till he should touch the American continent,
and then trend southward towards the new English
settlements in Virginia.   An alternative course pro-

posed by him, and one indeed that he most strongly favoured, was to go to the north-west and explore the region of Davis Strait; but this the ship's company rejected.

Once while heading towards Newfoundland Hudson saw a vessel sailing in the opposite direction and tried to speak her, but she kept away, probably fearing an encounter with one of the piratical vessels that sometimes sailed under the flag of the States General. Hudson gave chase, but being unable to overtake the stranger before night-fall, again turned to his westerly course. On the second of July he reached the grand banks of Newfoundland, nearly three months after leaving the Zuyder Zee. A fleet of French fishermen were on the banks, close followers of the earlier voyagers to the strange shores of the new world, and the forerunners of thousands of other hardy adventurers. Hudson did not attempt to hold any communication with them, but passed them at a little distance. Finding himself on soundings and becalmed he sought to divert the crew by giving them a day's fishing, and he set the whole ship's company to work with the lines, at which their success was so great that in a few hours they had taken between one and two hundred cod.

The calm on the fishing banks lasted two or three days, but after that a favourable wind helped the *Half Moon* on her way, and crippled though she was by the loss of her foremast, on the 15th of July she finally came in sight of the American coast. The fog now settled so heavily along the shore that Hudson did not dare proceed till it had lifted, but after two or three days a shift of weather enabled him to run into a deep bay about latitude thirty-four. Geographers have believed that this was Penobscot Bay, on the Maine coast. Into it ran a large river, the shores of which were covered with immense pine trees, which a familiar tradition tells us once extended in an almost unbroken belt along the whole length of the American coast. Of that great marginal forest little now remains except in the pine belt of the South and the lumber region of which the Penobscot is one of the centres.

Before entering the bay the *Half Moon* was visited by canoes bearing five or six savages, who were received on board, eating and drinking with the white men. They had already come in contact with French traders and could speak several words of their language. They appeared harmless and friendly, but the people of the *Half Moon* were not inclined to trust them. When the anchor was down other boats came alongside, some of them bringing furs of fine quality, which were offered in trade for articles of dress. It is said that some of the boats used by the Indians were shallops such as were made by the French.

For several days the sailors were employed on the shore in cutting and preparing a stick for a new foremast. The rigging of this spar took more time, and while the vessel was preparing to proceed upon her voyage and the last details were engrossing the attention of the master, there occurred a disgraceful incident which we must permit Robert Juet to relate.

> In the morning we manned our scute with four muskets and six men and took one of their shal·lops and took it aboard, then we manned our boat and scute with twelve men and muskets, and two stone pieces or murderers, and drove the salvages from their houses and took the spoil of them as they would have done of us.

" As they would have done of us "—no other palliation than that is offered for a crime as dastardly as it was unprovoked. The question whether Hudson gave any order or consent which would make him morally responsible for this outrage, will never be answered except by conjecture. Technically responsible as the master of the vessel he certainly was, but it must not be forgotten that he was then only the master on sufferance. He was riding a whirlwind, exploring strange seas with a half mutinous crew, leading by his seamanship and directing by the exercise of skill and diplomacy a pack of malcontents who simply permitted him to retain a nominal control of their actions while he pursued his explorations. This is not a fanciful view to take of the relations between Hudson and his crew. His mastery of them ended when he turned back at their dictation from the coast of Nova Zembla, and their influence over his fortunes was established when he asked and they granted their consent to continue the voyage. I see no other way to explain several of the events of the 1609 voyage than by

adopting the perfectly reasonable hypothesis that
Hudson was in reality navigating officer and pilot, but
not master of his crew. That he should have undertaken a voyage of discovery under such conditions
is marvellous, though it may be thought that the
result justified his judgment.

With such a ship's company there might be no
grave or immediate danger of actual outbreak against
authority so long as that authority was confined to
sailing orders and the usual discipline of the ship.
Sailors must live by work, and so long as the work is
not too hard, the restrictions not too many, the food
plenty, and the pay sure, one captain is as good as
another; indeed a captain who has asked permission
of his men to continue his voyage is much better than
another, because he dares not thwart them when they
wish to indulge in such pleasantries as firing upon
defenceless savages and pilfering unguarded wigwams.

Immediately after the outrage just recorded the sails
of the *Half Moon* were set and the voyage continued.
The theory suggested by Captain John Smith, namely
that south of Virginia there was a passage through the
continent to the Pacific Ocean, is supposed by several
writers to have taken possession of Hudson's mind.
There is no doubt that he possessed a previous knowledge of prominent points on the American coast, for
when he made his first landfall after leaving Penobscot
Bay, he confidently pronounced it Cape Cod. "This is
the headland," says Juet, "which Captain Bartholomew
Gosnold discovered in the year 1602 and called Cape

Cod because of the store of codfish that he found there-
about." In Juet's narrative at this point there is
some confusion as to latitude, a not uncommon fault
with sailors and geographers of that day. De Laet's
New World, published at Leyden in 1625, contains
a statement that does not fully agree with that of Hudson's clerk in regard to this part of the voyage; his
version, which has been supposed to have been drawn
from Hudson's personal account, is to the effect that
when the latter first saw land in latitude forty-one
degrees, forty-three minutes, he supposed it to be an
island and called it New Holland, but that he afterwards discovered it to be part of the continent and
identical with the Cape Cod of Gosnold. There is
even a slight doubt arising from the above-mentioned
confusion regarding latitude, whether Hudson really
saw Cape Cod at all, or only the south-west point of
Nantucket. Wherever or whatever the land before
him was, Hudson resolved to know something more
about it. He sent some of his men ashore in a boat,
not daring to venture in too near with his vessel. The
exploring party found bottom at five fathoms within a
bow shot of the shore; they then landed and discovered
among other things, "goodly grapes and rose trees
which they brought aboard." As he lay in very close
to the shore the following morning, Hudson thought
he heard a voice calling to them, and as his humanity
was stirred by the thought that some unfortunate
European might have been abandoned on that coast
and needed his assistance, he again had the boat

manned and sent ashore. The sailors were not successful in finding any white man, but coming across
some Indians, who appeared to be friendly, they
brought one of them to the vessel and gave him food
and presents. Juet is careful to note that these
savages had green tobacco which they smoked in
pipes of red clay with copper stems.

The voyage from Nantucket and Martha's Vineyard,
which Hudson appears to have sighted, was uneventful till about the middle of August, when the *Half
Moon* ran near the mouth of Chesapeake Bay. From
the entry in the journal we gather that the presence of
Englishmen in Virginia was well known to Hudson.
"This is an entrance to the Kings River in Virginia,"
he says, "where our Englishmen are." Newport was
in charge of a party that included Smith, Gosnold, and
others, with some of whom our navigator had personal
acquaintance. The *Half Moon* was encountering very
heavy weather when she arrived at the mouth of
Chesapeake Bay and it may have been that this prevented Hudson from attempting to find and converse
with his countrymen, yet this reason alone seems
hardly sufficient to account for his failure to make
any effort in that direction. It is more probable that,
having sought the neighbourhood of that settlement, he
turned away from it for other reasons than tempor-
ary stress of weather. We may surmise that one of
these reasons was born of his consciousness that in
serving the Dutch he had laid himself open to the
criticism of his English friends.

South-west from the Chesapeake for several days the *Half Moon* sailed, neither going very far nor accomplishing anything. In the latitude, as the journal makes it, of thirty-five degrees, forty-one minutes, Hudson reversed his course and ran north. One of his biographers says :

> The cause however is not difficult to conjecture, he had gone far enough to ascertain that the information given him by Captain Smith with respect to a passage into the Pacific south of Virginia was incorrect and he probably did not think it worth while to spend more time in so hopeless a search ; he therefore retraced his steps.

In another place the same writer laments that we have not the journal written by Hudson himself. " It is highly probable," he says, " that if the journal of the voyage had been kept by Hudson, we should have been informed of his reasons for changing the southerly course at this time." I suspect that the last thing that Hudson would have done would have been to give his reasons for the change of course. We have, it seems to me, strong grounds for conjecturing that he had sailed south partly to see Captain Smith and his companions. While still at a distance such a meeting promised only pleasure, but near at hand, having come to a sudden and somewhat shamefaced realisation of what that visit might involve and forming a resolution not to see them, he would find it necessary to divert the suspicion of his people from the real cause of what must have seemed a bootless and senseless change of plan. Thirty-five degrees and forty-five minutes is not very far down the North Carolina coast. Hudson did not sail as far south as Cape Hatteras and he certainly did not go far enough to determine that the information given him by Smith was incorrect.

CHAPTER VII

N the 28th of August, a hot and sultry midsummer day, the lower capes of what was subsequently known as Delaware Bay were passed, and Hudson saw the shores stretching away to the north-west; while towards the north-east he also descried land, which he at first took to be an island but afterwards found to be the upper point of the bay. We now know this point as Cape May.

As the *Half Moon* entered the bay, the tide ran strong and deep, and from the power of the current and the accumulation of sand in extensive shoals, the explorer made sure that a large stream flowed into it. A day was spent in sounding, which was an occupation of no little difficulty, and indeed danger, as the *Half Moon* was obliged to feel her way from one shallow to another, groping for the channels between them.

Turning to the journal of Juet for a description of the day's work, we read:

The eighth and twentieth fair and hot weather; a wind at south south-west; in the morning at six of the clock we weighed and steered away north twelve leagues till noon and came to the point of the land, and being hard by the land in five fathoms on the sudden we came into three fathoms; then we bore up and had but ten foot water and joined to the point; then as soon as we were over we had five, six, seven, eight, nine, ten, twelve, and thirteen fathoms; then we found the land to trend away north-west with a great bay and rivers. But the bay we found shoaled and in the offing we had ten fathoms and had sight of beaches and dry sand, then we were forced to stand back again, so we stood back south-east by south three leagues and by seven of the clock we anchored in eight fathoms of water and found a tide set to the north-west and north north-west; that riseth one fathom and floweth south south-east. He that will thoroughly discover this great bay must have a small pinasse that must draw up four or five foot water to sound before him. At five in the morning we weighed and steered away to the eastward not many courses, for the northern land is full of shoals. We went among them and one we struck and we went away and steered away to the south-east.

The ninth and twentieth fair weather, with some thunder and showers, the wind shifting between the south south-west and the north north-west. In the morning we weighed at the break of day and stood toward the northern land which we found to be all islands to our sight and great capes from them, and are shoaled three leagues off, for we going by them struck ground with our rudder. We steered off south-west one glass [*i. e.* one hour by the glass] and had five fathoms, then we

steered south-east three glasses, then we found
seven fathoms, then steered north-east by east four
leagues and came to twelve and thirteen fathoms. At one of the clock I went to the top-mast
head and set the land and the body of the islands
to appear north-west by north, and at four of the
clock we had gone four leagues east south-east,
and north-east by east, and found but seven fathoms; and it was calm so we anchored. Then I
went again to the top-mast head to see how far
I could see land about us, and could see no more
but the islands and the souther point of them, it
appeared, north-west by west eight leagues off, so
we rode till midnight; then the wind came to the
north north-west so we weighed and set sail. At
sunset the anchor was let go in eight fathoms.

There are parts of the foregoing entry that appear to
have been transcribed by Juet from Hudson's own
journal, and it is more than possible that most of Juet's
work was merely a rewriting, distinguished from the
original mainly by its omissions. A hot night succeeded the midsummer day, but during the night one
of the sudden thunderstorms that are characteristic of
this coast dispelled the heat and brought with it from
the land a sweet cool breeze that "refreshed the weary
men with the moist perfumes of sweet shrubs and summer flowers," to quote a well-known American biographer. At daybreak the anchor was got aboard and
the *Half Moon* resumed her explorations, but soon
grated on the sand again. By this time Hudson was
convinced that this shallow basin, with its constantly
recurring sand bars, could not possibly be the entrance

to such a strait as he wished to find ; he therefore left Delaware Bay, doubled Cape May, and again stood north.

Coasting what is now New Jersey he saw a shore that appeared sunken and dotted with small islands. The latest traveller along that shore must recognise the truth of the description, except that to modern eyes there appears an almost continuous line of cottages, with here and there a hotel to break the monotony. The first relief from that flat sandy prospect was afforded by the highlands of Navesink, that were seen early in the morning of the second of September, looming to the north-west. "It is a very good land to fall in with," exclaims Juet, "and a pleasant land to see."

The journalist thus described the approach to New York harbour :

> At three of the clock in the afternoon we came to three great rivers, so we stood along to the northermost, thinking to have gone into it, but we found it to have a very shoal bar before it, for we had but ten foot water ; then we cast about to the southward and found two fathoms, three fathoms, and three and one quarter, till we came to the south side of them ; then we had five and six fathoms and anchored. So we sent in our boat to sound and they found no less water than four, five, six, and seven fathoms and returned in an hour and a half. Here we weighed and went in and rode in five fathoms, oozy ground, and saw many salmona, mullets and rays very great. The height is forty degrees, thirty minutes.

Thus is recorded in technical and inartistic phrases

the commencement of one of the most notable voyages
of which we have knowledge. At daybreak on the
morning following the date of the foregoing entry, the
master of the *Half Moon*, seeing evidence of "good
rideing" further up the bay, again sent the ship's boat
ahead to sound the channel, and presently followed,
sailing close along shore for some distance. He finally came to an anchor close to the land, in the neighbourhood of an Indian encampment, from which anchorage the boat was sent ashore and the crew
went to fishing, making a great catch of mullet, etc.

The statement in the journal regarding the "three
rivers," that appeared to offer a triple choice for the
route of the *Half Moon* upon entering the bay below
Manhattan, cannot be explained at this late day, and
indeed it is doubtful if any historian in colonial times
could have thrown more light upon the subject.

There is a tradition to the effect that the first place
of landing was at Coney Island. John Romeyn Brodhead supposes the three rivers to have been "undoubtedly" the Raritan and the Narrows, and "probably"
Rockaway Inlet. The "high and pleasant land" of
Juet is set down by Dr. Asher as the south coast of
Staten Island. Nearly every biographer of Hudson
has agreed with one or the other of these theories,
though neither will bear the test of comparison with
the narrative. While the first entrance of the *Half
Moon* into the Hudson River must always be a subject
for speculation to the curious, it is quite possible that
the three rivers that Juet noticed no longer have a sep-

arate existence, and that therefore no amount of study
can ever result in a solution. It is well known that
several bars exist at the harbour entrance, in a line with
the point of Sandy Hook, so that vessels of deep
draught are obliged to find ingress and egress through
the channels that run between them. Nothing is more
usual, or indeed inevitable, than for such bars to change
their height and extent in the course of a few years. It
is more than possible that three hundred years ago the
sandbars at the mouth of the bay may have been above
water, just as Sandy Hook, which is of the same char·
acter, is to-day. Indeed there is no evidence that in
1609 Sandy Hook was the same in height as it is now.
The recorded changes of numerous sandy points on the
New Jersey and New England coasts within a generation would suggest a strong doubt that the point in
question can have remained unchanged in position and
character for three hundred years.

From the general description of the Navesink Highlands that the journal gives us, and the note relating
to the three rivers immediately following, it seems reasonable to suppose that some such theory as that I have
suggested may afford the true interpretation of a difficult passage. It is a most fortunate thing for mariners
that they are not obliged to beat about the entrances to
harbours and rivers they are inclined to enter till authors
have decided for them some knotty points of geography.
To the general reader these speculations are perhaps of
slight importance, the main fact being that Hudson
entered the river and commenced an examination of its

extent and characteristic features such as no previous navigator had attempted.

Wherever the first landing may have been, whether on the New Jersey shore, or upon Long Island, or Staten Island, or Coney Island, there are several un-equivocal statements that are not without interest. A good harbour, clear water, good fishing, and friendly natives summarise the favourable commencement of a propitious voyage.

There was at the outset one mishap, but fortunately not of a serious character. "At night the wind blew hard at the north-west," says Juet, "and our anchor came home and we drove on shore, but took no hurt, thanked be God, for the ground is soft sand and ooze." This entry evidently refers to the night of the third, though it is included in the record of the happenings of the following day. The direction of the wind, from the north-west, may give a hint of the anchorage of the *Half Moon* that night. If inside Sandy Hook she might well have been driven on soft ground by a stiff north-west wind, and it is hard to understand how the accident could have occurred at any other point.

On the fourth of September a number of red men came out in their canoes, ready to trade, bringing green tobacco, which they exchanged for glasses and beads. When we consider that the Indians of the Atlantic coast of America have never been known to be traders, the readiness with which they practised the art upon this occasion would seem to indicate previous tuition. Further up the river, we are informed, the savages came to the *Half Moon* bringing gifts. They were "very civil," according to Juet's story, and also well clad in garments of loose deerskin. Yellow copper, the possession of which by the Indians of Maine and Cape Cod has been spoken of, was again in evidence. In the arts of civilisation these people seem to have made a beginning, as shown not alone in their use of metal, but also in their ability to "make good bread" from the flour of the maize.

Juet mentions "maize or Indian wheat" and we are a little curious to know how he chanced upon the terms that were afterwards generally used by the colonists and are still employed to denote American corn.

The first landing in force by the people of the *Half Moon* seems to have been upon the morning of the fifth. They encountered a considerable number of friendly Indians, men, women, and children, who greeted them kindly, giving them tobacco. One man came aboard and brought dried currants, which Hudson [here the record seems to be a literal transcript from his log] found to be excellent, "sweet and good." Once more the narrator notes the abundance of copper, used in tobacco pipes and "in ornaments which they wore about their necks." The women brought hemp, and many of the men were dressed in mantles of feathers, while others wore skins and fine furs. It is evident, from the testimony at hand, that these poor savages appeared in their best finery, the court regalia of the forest. These details, minutely recorded as they are, seem to have made a strong and favourable impression upon the explorer; but Juet, in spite of the splendid appearance and exemplary conduct of the Indians, says, "we durst not trust them."

That was always the attitude of Juet and the crew—mistrust, misapprehension, and the cruelty that springs from misapprehension. Hudson alone seems to have trusted the savages and to have been trusted by them. His example is repeated in history. The same trust and corresponding confidence has since been displayed by Penn, by Roger Williams, by Sir William Johnson, by every broad-minded man who has dealt with the North American Indian. Men of small calibre have expected cruelty and treachery and they have received it, and shared its baleful effect with the communities in which they lived. Hudson, Penn, Williams, and Johnson have been pre-eminent among those who have received fair and even generous treatment from the red men.

The reason for Juet's distrust was inherent in the character of the men composing the crew of the *Half Moon*. In the morning they had gone ashore and had penetrated some distance into the oak woods, where it is quite improbable that they behaved themselves with any greater propriety or honesty than they had observed while in Penobscot Bay, as it has been the experience of the world that the leopard does not frequently change his spots. Hudson might well have doubted the Indians at that time; not from any evidence of treachery on their part, but because he knew the disposition of his own unruly crew and was assured that having permitted a firebrand to be sent ashore a conflagration would be the logical result.

That there was reason for apprehension the events of the following day proved. On the sixth of September, John Coleman, with whose name we are already familiar, was sent with four subordinate seamen in a boat to sound, the direction taken being probably through the Narrows. When the little party had gone far enough to discover the upper bay, or harbour, of New York, described as ''an open sea,'' they started to return with the encouraging report that the *Half Moon* might safely proceed. Before going far their boat was attacked by two canoes, a fight ensued, a flight of arrows proved more than a match for the clumsy firearms of the Europeans, and John Coleman was killed by a shaft which struck him in the throat.

Of the men who were with him two were severely, though not mortally, hurt. They managed to keep up a running fight till darkness gave them an opportunity to escape. The crippled crew, with their dead leader in the boat, cowered under the deep shade of the trees that overhung the shore, beset by perils which were magnified by their ignorant fears, and to which their experience could present no parallel.

It is difficult to imagine or portray a more doleful plight than that of these fugitive sailors—Englishmen or Dutchmen as you will—drifting down from danger to danger, unaware of the aversion of their savage foes to a nocturnal attack ; ignorant of their own position or that of the vessel. Rain fell, and the match, without which a musketeer of that day was helpless, was extinguished. The current ran swift and strong ; they put out their grapnel and it would not hold.

So they drifted forlornly till morning, when they saw the vessel in the distance, but made such slow progress in reaching her that it was only two hours before noon when they came alongside and were hoisted aboard.

Coleman was buried ashore upon a point that Hudson named in his honour "Coleman's Point." The Coleman's Point of the seventeenth century Dutch maps was on the end of Sandy Hook, but there is no strong evidence that the *Half Moon* was near Sandy Hook at the time of his burial, and indeed it has been repeatedly shown that little reliance can be placed upon the accuracy, in their minor details, of the Dutch maps of the New World.

There is a legend, more or less in accord with accepted facts, that presents the Indian's point of view regarding the appearance of the *Half Moon* in the mouth of the Hudson River.

Some red men, so the tale runs, were quietly fishing, somewhere between Manhattan Island and the ocean, when one of them discovered upon the horizon an object that filled them with amazement. It suggested an enormous bird, and such they were at first inclined to think it. No doubt their lines, or whatever equivalent in pine-root fibre or deer sinew answered the pur-

pose of lines, were quickly drawn in and their stone
anchor got aboard, while they debated the wisdom
or use of instant flight. Gigantic birds were unheard
of on that coast, and the appearance of one from
the seaward side must portend some supernatural
event.

After a while there arose a dispute, a difference of
opinion between the occupants of the canoe. What
had at first seemed to be a bird soon suggested some
sort of a wigwam, of architectural style not hitherto
known to the simple savage, but not impossibly like
the sort of house he might dream of inhabiting when
he had attained the happy hunting grounds to which
every good Indian expects to go. The house idea
rather gained ground. One of the fishermen suggested
that it might be a wigwam in a canoe, but a canoe of
such size and a house of such capacity as no man had
ever seen before.

Clearly this vast structure, that came towards the
fascinated occupants of the canoe like a thing of life,
riding the waves without the use of a paddle, and
looming more and more as it approached, could be
none other than the abode, or at least the vehicle, of
the Manitou.

The watchers of this marvellous apparition were
divided between fear, curiosity, duty—would it be wise
to wait till it came nearer, or prudent to flee to the
forest-lined shore, or patriotic to warn the chiefs of
their people of the portent ? While they lingered they
discovered that there were living creatures, men evi-

dently, on the object that they had agreed was a monster canoe.

They finally agreed to retreat and paddled with all speed for the shore, and ere long all the people on Manhattan were informed of the approach of the gods, for the chiefs sent out swift runners to call in the hunters and to gather the members of the different villages.

At last the great ark drew near the shore. There had been a mighty debate before the sachem had settled what was to be done, one party counselling flight and concealment, while the other argued that if it was a manitou such precautions would serve no purpose whatever save to offend him ; but the question had been speedily settled, and when the *Half Moon* came to an anchor all the population of Manhattan was congregated on what is now the Battery to hail and bid it welcome.

From the great canoe a smaller one was lowered into the water and into this descended the supreme Manitou, clad in a gorgeous coat of scarlet, with lacings of some substance brighter even than the copper of which the Indian's pipes and ornaments are made. This august personage was accompanied by several others, more soberly dressed, who were no doubt inferior manitous. The sachem met the lesser canoe on its arrival at the beach and treated its occupants with ceremonious courtesy. They had for the occasion donned their official and gala finery of feather robes and headdresses, cloaks of rare furs, and ornaments of glittering copper. It is somewhat difficult to imagine

whether they or the chief Manitou in his scarlet and
gold made the more gorgeous appearance.

When the great personage was safely landed and had
been received according to approved ceremonial usage,
he caused to be lifted from the canoe a vessel the like
of which no one had ever seen before, and out of it he
poured into a smaller but equally curious receptacle
some liquid that had a strange but not unpleasant
odour.   Taking this in his hand and inclining his head
to the company, he drank a little of the contents and
handed it to the nearest chief, who carefully smelled of
it and passed it, untasted, to his nearest neighbour.   He
in turn lifted the cup to his nose and offered it, without
drinking of its contents, to the chief next to him.   So
around the circle went the first flowing bowl ever
offered by way of a convivial treat on Manhattan
Island.   The custom has since been somewhat abused.
Indian after Indian, teetotallers till that day, sniffed and
declined, till the last man, who should have passed the
liquor again to their entertainer, wavered and made a
speech.   With the glass of rum in his hand he har-
angued the assembled braves and sachems, and there
was a curious mixture of Tammany acumen and Roman
heroism in his words.   The substance of his speech,
translated into English, was somewhat as follows:

If this singular thing, which is neither a shell
nor yet a grape leaf, but which is capitally con-
trived to hold a liquor which hath a most admirable and seductive odour, is handed back to the
great and powerful Manitou who hath poured it

out for us and who hath himself partaken of it, no
doubt he will be offended and may visit upon us
some terrible calamity.   It will be far better for
one man to risk death than for all the tribe to be
wiped out.   I will drink this unknown concoction
and if I die you may put upon my monument,
" He died for his country."

At least if those were not the exact words used by
the Indian, that is about what his speech amounted to.
It would have been admirable merely as a sentiment.
Put into action it was sublime.   He raised the cup to
his lips and drank every drop, though the fiery stuff
burned his throat and the tears came to his eyes.   He
was willing to perish for his tribe, surely he could en-
dure choking for them.

With awestruck faces the Indians gathered closer to
watch their companion and champion.   For a few mo-
ments they saw no change in him ; then suddenly it
was noticed that his eyes gazed unsteadily upon them;
he swayed from side to side ; presently he sank to the
ground and lay as one dead.

Now if the man in the red coat had not been regarded as a manitou, it is probable that the whole history of Henry Hudson would have ended at this point
and would ere this have been forgotten.   Believing him
to be superhuman, his red hosts waited and after a time
their companion revived.   He declared in accents of
unmistakable conviction, but in language that unfortunately has not been preserved, that he never had
such a good time in his life.   He wanted some more of
the same seductive liquor.

Seeing how good a thing this rum seemed to be, the other Indians changed their minds and were soon on the highway to intoxication. The pow-wow ended in an orgie, and when the Manitou returned to his wigwam in the big canoe the entire tribe wanted to see him home.

In the archives of the New York Historical Society may be found all the main incidents of this tradition, as it was furnished a century or more ago by men of reputation and undoubted veracity, who wrote it verbatim as it was told then by the Indians whose forefathers inhabited Manhattan about the year 1609.   As set down here nothing of the story may be claimed as original by the present writer.   In concluding it let me quote from a paper deposited with the New York Historical Society by the Rev. Samuel Miller, D.D., who received it from the Rev. John Hackewelder, who got the matter contained in it from the Indians of the Delaware nation in the eighteenth century.

After this general intoxication had ceased (during which time the whites had confined themselves to their vessel) the man with the red clothes returned to them again and distributed presents among them, to wit, beads, axes, hoes, stockings, etc. They (the Indians) say that they had become familiar to each other, and were made to understand by signs that they now would return home, but would visit them next year again, when they would bring them more presents and stay with them awhile; but as they could not live without eating, they should then want a little land of them to sow seeds in order to raise herbs to put in their broth. That the vessel returned the season following and they were much rejoiced at seeing each other; but that the whites laughed at them, seeing they knew not the use of the axes, hoes, etc., that they had given them, they having had these hanging to their breasts as ornaments; and the stockings they had made use of as tobacco pouches. The whites now put handles, or helves, in the former, and cut trees down before their eyes and dug the ground, and showed them the use of the stockings. Here (say they) a general laughter ensued among them (the Indians) that they had remained for so long a time ignorant of the use of so valuable implements, and had borne with the weight of such heavy metal hanging to their necks for such a length of time. They took every white man they saw for a manitou, yet inferior to the supreme Manitou, to wit, to the one that wore the red and laced clothes. Familiarity daily increasing between themselves and the whites, the latter now proposed to stay with them, asking only for so much land as the hide of a bullock would cover (or encompass) which hide was brought forward and spread on the ground before them. That they readily granted this request; whereupon the whites took a knife and beginning at one place on this hide cut it up into a rope not thicker than the finger of a little child, so that by the time this hide was cut up there was a great heap. That this rope was drawn out to a great distance and then brought round again, so that the ends might meet. That they carefully avoided its breaking, and that upon the whole it encompassed a large piece of ground. That they (the Indians)

were surprised at the superior wit of the whites,
but did not wish to contend with them about a
little land, as they had enough. That they and
the whites lived for a long time contentedly together, although these asked from time to time
more land of them ; and proceeding higher and
higher up the Mahicanittuk (Hudson River), they
believed they would soon want all their country,
and which at that time was the case.

In Yates and Moulton's *History of New York* there
is an account of this legend which may be taken as a
corroborative.   On page 257 of the first edition of that
interesting though never completed work will be found
this paragraph.

> Mr. Heckewelder received the tradition about
> sixty-five years ago, and took it down verbatim,
> as it was related to him by aged and respected
> Delawares, Monseys, and Mahicanni.   Dr. Barton
> says the story is told in the same way by all the
> Indians of the tribes of Delawares, the " Monces,"
> and " Mohiccans " ; and in relating the incidents
> they laugh at their own ignorance.   But what still
> further shows (says Dr. Barton) that considerable
> dependence may be placed upon the tradition is
> this, that to this day the Delawares, the Monseys,
> and the Mohiccans call New York Manahachtani-
> enks, that is, the place at which we were drunk.

Singularly this is not the only nor the best authenti-
cated story connecting Hudson's voyage with a scene
of debauchery.   If not absolute proof, there is at least
ground for a strong suspicion that the Master of the
Half Moon introduced fire-water among the Indians,

yet it must be remembered that there is no word in the above tradition to show definitely that the manitou in the red and laced coat was Henry Hudson. There are indeed several details, and particularly that of the second visit in the following year, that could not possibly refer to Hudson. If there is any truth in the legend, it is probable that the Indians in transmitting it gradually jumbled several traditions, and may have had a composite hero owing some feature to every visitor from Verrazzano to the early Dutch settlers on Manhattan. Further accounts of the introduction of rum to the Indians will be given in their appropriate places in this narrative.

CHAPTER VIII

FTER the burial of Coleman on the point of land which Juet describes, the Master of the *Half Moon* caused the boat to be hoisted aboard, and taking waste boards built up the bulwarks of the vessel into a sort of barricade, behind which the men could move without danger from the direct arrows of the savages.

The following night a watch was strictly kept while the ship rode at her anchor, but nothing occurred to disturb the voyagers. It is now well known that even when inclined to be hostile the Indian seldom attacks at night; a fact perhaps partly due to his intense superstition, not less than that which Stevenson attributes to the inhabitants of the South Sea Islands, which peoples the night with ghosts and hob-goblins. This may have been a reason for the quiet enjoyed by Hudson and his men that summer night, but the chances are that the men who had killed Coleman were of a different tribe from the peaceful Raratans who then occupied the shores nearest to the *Half Moon*, and

that there was actually no reason for apprehension.
There was one fact of which Hudson and his company
could not have had cognisance, well known though
it was to the men who settled the shores of the North
River a few years later. That was the diverse character of different tribes and sub-tribes of Indians inhabiting the shores of the great stream. Some of the
savages were fierce and warlike, others of a peaceable and more kindly disposition. Some lived by
rapine and bred their young braves almost exclusively
to a knowledge of predatory tactics, to extreme hardi-
ness of body and violence of temper. They were
the bandits of the woods, robbers from the cradle, who
hunted the wild beasts of the forest or the men of
the neighbouring villages with equal zest. In contrast
to these fierce tribes, both in mode of life and disposition, were the friendly fishermen, the tillers of the
ground and dredgers for oysters, who afforded what the
others considered their legitimate prey. Had Hudson
understood this distinction he would not have been
surprised that one party of savages should have set
upon his boat and murdered one of his men, while
another company, a few hours later, visited his vessel
with every sign of friendliness and showed no knowledge of the outrage. It was perhaps not easy to comprehend the fact that villages on opposite sides of the
stream, or even within a few miles of each other upon
the same side, not only held no communication with
each other but were actually at bitter enmity.

When the morning came the canoes began to

approach as before and the red men showed an evident desire to trade. Hudson never seems to have felt that distrust of them, or suspicion regarding their motives that Juet and the crew exhibited. The latter indeed hatched a very pretty plot to detect the guilt of the murderers, should they be among the visitors who were admitted to the *Half Moon* that morning. They displayed the boat in which Coleman was killed with the red evidence of the tragedy still apparent in it and watched the Indians narrowly to see whether they would show by any signs that they understood what had occurred. It was very much like the ordeal of touch which superstition for centuries prescribed for the detection of a murderer. Juet's account is as follows : " So we fitting up our boat did marke them to see if they would make any show of the death of our man ; *which they did not.*"

The Indians brought tobacco and corn to barter for knives or ornaments and showed a friendly attitude, which, however, did not allay the suspicion of Hudson's people. They were always upon the lookout for treachery, and like most suspicious people found what to them were convincing indications of an unfriendly spirit. Two canoes came out to the vessel on the second morning after Coleman's burial and it was noticed that while the Indians in one of the boats "made a show of buying knives to betray us," those who filled the other had bows and arrows among them.

It was always the policy of Juet and his shipmates when they saw, or imagined they saw, any indications of ill will to strike first. Whether Hudson upon this occasion shared their suspicions we cannot tell. He probably gave at least a tacit consent to their action. There is no evidence or even claim that the Indians used their bows or arrows in a hostile manner, but no sooner did they draw alongside of the *Half Moon* than the white men captured two of them and detained them on board, preventing the others from coming onto the ship. The hostages were for some unexplained reason made to put on red coats, probably for the diversion of the crew, to whom such horseplay may be supposed to have afforded amusement, though possibly a more diplomatic reason may be assigned for what seems to have been a very childish proceeding.

Another canoe approaching the *Half Moon*, which still swung at her anchor not far from shore, one of its occupants was shanghaied aboard while the other was ordered to go about his business, but the last captive escaped his tormentors, and, springing upon the bulwarks, leaped overboard. Up to this time no attack upon the vessel had been made or attempted. The Indians, who seem to have been impelled mainly by curiosity and a desire to barter, came without evil intentions and went without any difficulty, even when their companions were detained by the Europeans. But now, having worked themselves to a pitch of suspicion for which their own ill-advised actions had given ample cause, the people of the *Half Moon* weighed and stood out towards the channel, where they again dropped anchor and remained for that night.

"The tenth, fair weather," wrote Juet, "we rode still till twelve of the clock. Then we weighed and went over and found it shoal all the middle of the river, for we could find but two fathoms and a half and three fathoms for the space of a league; then we came to three fathoms and four fathoms and so to seven fathoms, and anchored." Moulton gives the location of this shoal and anchorage as the east sand bank in the Narrows, than which no more probable solution of the account has been offered.

Although September with its cool nights was now a third gone, our navigator found the heat at times sufficiently intense to be noted. Beyond the statement that the eleventh was fair and very hot weather, the journal gives no account of that day except as to varied soundings. At nightfall they made a good harbour, safe in all winds, and again anchored, and immediately the natives began to come out to them in their canoes, "making great show of love and gave us tobacco and Indian wheat, and departed for that night; but we durst not trust them."

Nothing of particular moment occurred during the night, and the morning dawned calm and hot. During the forenoon, while the *Half Moon* was still at her anchorage, a large fleet consisting of twenty-eight canoes filled with men, women, and children, approached from the shore. "To betray us," was Juet's ready comment, though it is difficult to imagine that

Indians upon a warlike, or even a menacing, expedition would take with them their women and children. "We saw their intent," says the journalist, "and suffered none of them to come aboard of us. At twelve of the clock they departed."

In this connection it is pertinent to quote from a footnote in Dr. Asher's invaluable treatise on Hudson. He says:

> Hudson himself, in the few scraps of the original logbook preserved by De Laet, and also in the communications which Van Meteren seems to have received from him, always speaks kindly of the North American Indians. He and his crew entirely disagreed with regard to the treatment due to the poor natives; and his kindness was rewarded by friendship, their sullen mistrust by acts of hostility. The poor Indian has but too often been thus both ill-treated and ill-judged by prejudiced Europeans.

This estimate, we must not forget, is from the pen of a foreign writer, with whom perhaps few Americans will entirely agree. We have our prejudices against the red man, and they are generally stronger and perhaps better founded than those of Europeans; but the careful student has long recognised that there were degrees of savagery in the aboriginal American, as there are in the aboriginal African or the aboriginal South Sea Islander; all were not alike cruel, selfish, warlike, or bloodthirsty.

We cannot point with any degree of certainty to the spot where the *Half Moon* spent the night of the 12th

of September, 1609, but could we do so we might conjecture to what tribe the Indian visitors belonged and
in a manner estimate the danger to which Hudson and
his crew may have been exposed.   Supposing that
the passage of the Narrows had been made and the
anchorage was in the upper bay, there is still the
unsettled question which was the nearest shore.   If
the vessel lay in the neighbourhood of the present Bay
Ridge or near Gowanus Bay, on the Long Island
shore, then the Canarse or some other tribe of the
Delaware stock were probably their visitors; fishermen, wampum makers, peaceable folk who lived rather
by trade than war, though their cousins upon the
western shore of the river were notable warriors.   If
the anchorage was over towards Bayonne or Bergen,
on the opposite side of the bay, the peaceful Raratans,
their first visitors [according to Moulton and O'Cal-
laghan], filled the eight and twenty canoes that threw
Juet and the crew into such a panic.   The inhabitants
of Manhattan were more fierce, a people dreaded by
their neighbours because of their predatory habits,
though the evidence at command does not show
them to have been particularly unfriendly either
towards Hudson or the later Dutch settlers.

Juet's note of the tide or current on the morning of
the twelfth, that it "floweth south-east by south
within," leads us to think that they had anchored in
the upper part of the Narrows near the present quaran-
tine station, though this is merely conjecture.   His account of the articles brought by the Indians for traffic,

oysters and beans, points a suggestion that they were either off Staten Island or Long Island. The first mention made in this chronicle of earthenware vessels, " great pots of earth to dress their meats in," occurs in the meagre narrative of the twelfth. At two o'clock of that day, having a fair tide though an uncertain wind, Hudson weighed anchor, and crossing the bay, entered the river and ascended several miles, coming to an anchor possibly about the foot of the present Forty-second Street. From there at seven in the morning with a brisk northerly wind, the explorer resumed his voyage, taking advantage of the last of the flood tide. In spite of the adverse wind the *Half Moon* made another four miles before the tide failed her and her next halting place is supposed to be just above where Grant's Tomb now overlooks the river. From where the traveller on the river now sees the viaduct, barges, and floats at Manhattanville, the long lines of freight cars at the river edge, and the beautiful heights beyond them crowned with monuments and buildings that are world famous, Hudson saw an unbroken forest of gigantic trees coming down to the very margin of the river and reflected in its unpolluted waters. That forest remained practically unbroken, save for an occasional clearing, till the dark days when the British army occupied New York during the revolution. Then the timber was hewn to afford fuel for the garrison.

Along the western bank of the river a similar forest spread, a forest that has excited the wonder and admiration of many a traveller. "Throughout the whole country," says O'Callaghan, "vegetation was rapid and all the natural productions luxuriant, owing to the constant decomposition of vegetable matter— plants, wild grass, and the deciduous foliage—which, annually dying, furnished an ever renewing supply of rich manure." Oaks, we are told, reached sixty or seventy feet without a knot. Chestnut, hickory, walnut, beech, butternut, buttonwood, birch, elm, pine, maple, ash, cedar, spruce, hemlock, poplar, willow, and many other native American trees, contributed to form the billowy masses of foliage that attracted the thoughtful master of the *Half Moon*. "Here are timbers for ships and wood for casks," he said.

The forests were full of luxuriant vines ; grapes hung in innumerable clusters from the boughs, and along the more precipitous hillsides, where the trees could not find foothold, the netted stalks of berry bushes grew, blackberries, raspberries, and numerous unknown varieties. Sweet and clean, the September air blew through miles upon miles of ripening fruits and nuts. Looking south Hudson saw stretching away that wonderful sheet of water that has been called the most beautiful bay in the world ; and to the north his eye ranged the vista beyond the unique bosses of the Palisades. It was a place and a time where even a prosaic and unimaginative man must have felt a quickening of the pulse and cherished at least a glim- mering inspiration of prophecy ; and Hudson, as we know, was not prosaic or unimaginative ; he was a follower of that will-o'-the-wisp that Cabot set afloat, a man to risk his life for a theory. Somewhere between the ragged heights of Weehawken and the commanding slope of Fort Washington, on the morning of the thirteenth of September, 1609, Henry Hudson stood on the deck of the *Half Moon* and knew that though the fates had warred against him, though the course that he had engaged to sail had not been accomplished, though he had come thus far only by the fickle favour of a mutinous crew, though he was master of his vessel only in name—yet he had not failed. He knew this, I say, because no man alive could look upon that scene, cherishing the knowledge that his report would reveal it to the world, and not be assured of immortal renown.

Four canoes came to the ship as soon as she had cast anchor, but none of their occupants was suffered to set foot on board, though they appeared to be friendly and brought stores to barter. In particular they had great numbers of very good oysters which they sold ''for trifles.''

With the turn of the tide that evening the voyage recommenced. The *Half Moon* went in with the flood six or seven miles and came to an anchor, as it is supposed, near Spuyten Duyvil. Here, according to the journal, she had '' five fathoms soft oozie ground ; and had an high point of land which showed out to us, bearing north by east five leagues off us.''

It should be noted that throughout the journal there is no question as to the character of the stream upon which Hudson was sailing. ''We entered the river,''

"We sailed up the river," "The river is full of fish." There is not even a hint that it was looked upon as a possible strait or channel between two seas. From the beginning to the end of the exploration Hudson must have known, and by this evidence he did know, that he was exploring a river. The claim, so frequently repeated, that this astute navigator was deceived into thinking that he had found the long-expected passage to the Indies, and reluctantly abandoned the idea only when the shoal water above Albany made further advance impossible, is a venerable but not very cunningly devised fable. Hudson knew, what his biographers should have discovered long ago, that he was no longer looking for the promised passage : he abandoned that search, for the time being at least, when he compromised with his rebellious people. What he was trying to do was to make his defeat spell victory, and the fact that he succeeded shows that his wisdom, perseverance, and tact were unexcelled even by his courage and devotion.

Nothing could be more meagre, more disappointing, than the journal's account of the stretch of river between Spuyten Duyvil Creek and the entrance to the Highlands. Certainly no one on board the *Half Moon* had ever seen a stream of equal volume and beauty, nor a landscape of more exquisite loveliness, than that which was presented to their eyes as they passed the unique structure of the Palisades and entered the open water of the Tappan Zee ; but no expression of wonder or admiration escaped master or men so far as the record informs us.

> In the night (of the thirteenth) I set the varia-
> tions of the compasse and found it to be thirteen
> degrees. In the afternoon we weighed, and turned
> in with the flood two leagues and a half further,
> and anchored all night ; and had five fathoms soft
> oozie ground ; and had an high point of land
> which showed out to us, bearing north and by
> east five leagues off us.

There is every probability that the high point of land noted was that which used to be known as Indian Head, the highest crest upon the line of the Palisades until the dynamite of a never-to-be-forgiven contractor destroyed it.   Assuming this to be the headland noted in the journal, we may take up the soulless narrative again, as follows :

> The fourteenth, in the morning, being very fair
> weather, the wind south-east, we sailed up the
> river twelve leagues, and had five fathoms and five
> fathoms and a quarter less ; and came to a streight
> between two points, and had eight, nine and ten
> fathoms ; and it trended north-east by north, one
> league ; and we had twelve, thirteen, and fourteen
> fathoms.

Let us take breath again and see where this uneventful chronicle has carried us. In Yates's and Moulton's history we find that the "streight between two points" is set down as the passage between Stony and Verplanck's Points.   This interpretation, which is generally followed, may be correct, though the words of the

journal seem open to another reading. After crossing
the Tappan Zee the *Half Moon* came between Teller's
or Croton Point and the high bluffs between Hook
Mountain and Haverstraw. It seems hardly possible
that even the prosaic Juet could have refrained from a
reference to so notable a land-mark as High Tor,
though he may have done so, even as he neglected
to observe the lake-like expanse of the Zee of Tappan.
With the evidence at hand I believe the "streight
between two points" to have been between Croton and
Point no Point.

"The river is half a mile broad," says the journal.
"Near Peekskill," comments Dr. Asher, echoing
Moulton, "there is very high land." "We went up
North West a league and a half, deep water," adds
Juet. "Then north-east by north, five miles (between
Stony Point and Peekskill?); then north-west by
north, two leagues, and anchored. The land grew
very high and mountainous. The river is full of fish."

We may now suppose the explorer to be in the
immediate neighbourhood of West Point. His queer
little Vlie-boat dropped her anchor in water that has
been celebrated by poets, pictured by artists, raved
over by generations of travellers, boasted about by
myriads of Americans—and her master, if he had any
reflections on the beauty of the scene, kept them to
himself; while his clerk sagely recorded that the river
was full of fish. The reason for this apathy was a
simple one. Hudson and his men were no better
nor worse in this respect than nearly all other men,

seamen or landsmen, of their time. There was no popular appreciation of beauty in landscape. The note
had not been struck. Artists used trees, mountains,
or water generally as accessories to figure composition,
and rarely showed by any sympathetic rendition of
landscape an appreciation of its beauty. Poets sang
feelingly of the sweetness and delicacy of flowers, but
seldom of the grandeur of the mountains, the charm of
the streams, or the solemnity of the forests. These
things, if noticed at all, were referred to solely as a
background for the human interest of their poems.
The Turners and Cunninghams, the Scotts and the
Corots, the Bryants and the Burroughses, all came afterwards. A taste for beauty in landscape is all a matter
of cultivation, and in 1609 it had not begun to be
cultivated. The average man of that day could no
more go into raptures over the beauty of the Highlands, than a Hottentot could be expected to discover a heaven of delight in the Ninth Symphony.

It was a misty morning, that fifteenth of September, when the dawn disclosed the shadowy outlines
of the Highlands to Hudson and his people; but after
the sun rose the mist cleared away and a fair southerly
breeze sprang up, propitious for the voyage. So the
anchor was got aboard and the voyagers proceeded,
we may well believe, with eyes open to all the material
advantage that might be derived from the water-way
they followed and the shores that enclosed them.
Everywhere the abundant forests promised a plentiful
supply of useful timber, the beetling crags on either

side suggested mineral wealth, while the teeming fish in the river called forth frequent expressions of surprise and delight.

During the passage through the Tappan Zee and the Highlands the *Half Moon* had carried the two captives taken further down the river, and dressed, it will be remembered, in red coats. Now as the voyage was continued with a fair wind through the Highlands, the watchfulness of the captors relaxed and somewhere about the vicinity of Cornwall or Newburgh the savages found opportunity to leap overboard and swim ashore. They did not omit, following the traditions of their race, to shout back expressions of insult and defiance, which the Europeans could not fail to comprehend, even though they did not understand the language from which the terms of contumely were chosen.

Through their wanton cruelty the crew of the *Half Moon* had involved themselves in a quarrel, the consequences of which might have been, and very nearly were, exceedingly serious. We have no means of knowing to what tribe the Indian prisoners belonged, but from what followed it seems fair to presume that they were members of one of the more warlike families, probably Mohawks. It seems certain that as soon as they reached the shore they lost no time in making good their threats by collecting a force of their fierce clansmen to watch the river shore for the return of the *Half Moon*, and to repay with violence the indignities to which they had been subjected. If they had ever

entertained an opinion that the white men were manitous, familiarity had undeceived them.

Towards night "we came to other mountains which
lie from the river's side." Here is undoubtedly the
first mention made by any European of the Catskill
Mountains. Nothing is said of the general contour of
the land beyond this brief mention, but an interesting
human note is added. "There wee found very loving
people and very old men." One of the best accounts
of the Indian tribes inhabiting the shores of the Hudson River is that given in 1846 by Dr. O'Callaghan,
who had ransacked all previous sources of information
on this subject when he wrote his celebrated history of
New Netherland. As it is not possible to improve
upon his summary, I quote it here without further
apology.

> The richness of the soil and the abundance of
> game favoured particularly the maintenance and in-
> crease of the savage race which occupied the coun-
> try at the time of Hudson's visit. These people,
> though belonging to the common stock of the
> Algonkin Lenape family, were cut up and divided
> into a number of separate or independent tribes or
> nations. To the east dwelt the Pequods and the
> Wampanoags, while the North River was divided
> between the terrible Maquaas, or Mohawks, who
> occupied its upper waters and imposed tribute on
> the surrounding tribes, the Machicanders, or river
> Indians, who lined its banks on either side to its
> mouth, and the Matouwacks of Sewan-hacky, or
> Long Island, who exercised jurisdiction over thir-
> teen minor tribes thereabout.

Beginning then with the Mohawks; these occupied the country on the west bank of the Cohotatea or Hudson River, from the head of navigation back, some seventy miles. Opposite to them, to the east, the wigwams of the Mohegans stretched beyond the mountains to the Connecticut. South of this nation were settled the Waraonkins on the east and the Waranancongyns on the west, in the vicinity of Esopus, where they were afterwards known as the Wappingi or Wappingers.

For the rest Dr. O'Callaghan devotes pages to their record, but they are not immediately pertinent to this narrative. Enough has been borrowed from this source to show that the "very loving people and very old men" of Juet's account were probably one of the northern sub-tribes of the "Mahicanders or River Indians," settled about where the present city of Catskill lies.

In the vicinity of Catskill the boat of the *Half Moon* was manned and went to fish, catching a "great store of good fish," but when in the morning the crew tried their luck on the same ground it proved indeed to be but "fisherman's luck," which they explained on the ground that the Indians had been fishing there all night. The weather was then fair and hot. The canoes of the savages began early in the morning to visit the ship and brought ears of Indian corn, pompions [pumpkins?], and tobacco. These things were purchased at a trifling cost, buttons and beads being accepted as medium of exchange, and a knife being considered equivalent to the value of the rarest furs.

Here the *Half Moon* rode all day.   Hudson took the
opportunity afforded to send ashore for a supply of
fresh water.   At nightfall he weighed anchor and
ascended the river five or six miles farther, where,
finding shoaling water, he again anchored.

At sunrise on a hot morning (September 16th) the
explorer again set sail and tried the channel for fifteen
or twenty miles farther, sounding as he went and finding numerous bars and islands, but a fair channel on
both sides.   In the course of the day he ran close to
the shore and grounded, and then having warped off
by the use of his small anchor, he came to grief on
some shoals on the opposite side of the channel, but
when the flood ran he heaved off again and having
reached a secure anchorage, rode all night.

This anchorage has been variously estimated to have
been somewhere between Castleton and Hudson.
There is no definite evidence on the subject beyond
what is here set down, and the reader has abundant
opportunity to settle the question of the exact locality
for himself.   The author has no hesitation in confessing that he cannot decide the question.

" Our master's mate," says Juet, " went ashore in
the morning with an old savage."   The historians
who have treated of this matter have assumed that
Hudson went ashore at this time.   We have his own
word for it that he went ashore at one time and was
treated with due consideration, and it is not really
important to an understanding of either the man or
his achievements to decide whether his visit to the

savages upon their own ground occurred at one or another particular point upon the river.

The old savage referred to above was one of the chiefs of the country, his subjects or tribesmen living somewhere about Albany.   He took the white man to his wigwam and made him welcome to the best cheer that he could offer.   Hudson's own account of his landing, at a point never determined, may well be introduced here.

> When I came on shore the swarthy natives all stood around and sung in their fashion.   [If John De Laet is to be credited, these were Hudson's own words.]   Their clothing consisted of the skins of foxes and other animals, which they dress and make the skins into garments of various sorts. Their food is Turkish wheat (maize, or Indian corn) which they cook by baking, and it is excellent eating.   They all came on board, one after another, in their canoes, which are made of a single hollowed tree ; their weapons are bows and arrows pointed with sharp stones, which they fasten with hard resin.   They had no houses but slept under the blue heavens, sometimes on mats of bulrushes interwoven, and sometimes on the leaves of trees.   They always carry with them all their goods, such as food and green tobacco, which is strong and good for use.   They appear to be a friendly people, but have a great propensity to steal, and are exceedingly adroit in carrying away whatever they take a fancy to.

In another place he is quoted as saying :

> It is as pleasant a land as one need tread upon.

Very abundant in all kinds of timber suitable for
ship-building and for making large casks or vats.
The people had copper tobacco pipes, from which
I inferred that copper might naturally exist there ;
and iron likewise according to the testimony of the
natives, who however did not understand preparing it for use. . . . I sailed to the shore in
one of their (the Indian's) canoes, with an old man
who was chief of a tribe consisting of forty men
and seventeen women.   These I saw there in a
house well constructed of oak bark and circular in
shape, so that it had the appearance of being well
built, with an arched roof. It contained a great
quantity of maize or Indian corn, and beans of the
last year's growth and there lay near the house for
the purpose of drying enough to load three ships,
besides what was growing in the fields.   On our
coming into the house, two mats were spread to sit
upon and immediately some food was served in
well-made red wooden bowls ; two men were also
dispatched at once with bows and arrows in quest
of game, who soon after brought in a pair of
pigeons which they had shot.   They likewise
killed a fat dog and skinned it in great haste with
shells which they had got out of the water.   They
supposed that I would remain with them for the
night, but I returned after a short time on board
the ship. The land is the finest for cultivation
that I ever set foot upon in my life, and it also
abounds in trees of every description.   The
natives are a very good people, for when they
saw that I would not remain, they supposed
that I was afraid of their bows, and taking the
arrows they broke them in pieces and threw
them into the fire.

These words are interesting if regarded merely as a graphic description of the savages that Hudson found upon the shores of the great river. They become doubly so when we consider that, if authentic, they form probably the longest and most fully detailed statement in regard to his travels that has been preserved of all that Hudson may have said or written. Speculation is stimulated. We are eager to know whether De Laet copied the words from some lost manuscript or transcribed and translated them from the spoken words of the navigator. That they were not transliterated sentences is certain—about the only thing sure in the whole matter—for De Laet wrote in Dutch and Hudson spoke only in English. There is every evidence that Hudson never visited Holland after he explored the Hudson. If De Laet saw him and conversed with him it must have been in England, in the months that intervened between the return of the *Half Moon* and the commencement of the fatal 1610 voyage. This does not seem probable, and indeed the whole style of the quotation is rather that of written than spoken words. The unanswered and perhaps unanswerable question is whether the style is De Laet's or Hudson's.

A more important question, also unanswered to this day, is whether (supposing De Laet drew from a written source his description of Hudson's voyage up the North River of New Netherland) that source is still waiting, undiscovered but undestroyed, for the eye and hand of some happy historian who may use it for the correction of errors into which many of us who have tried to tell the story of Hudson's voyages have been innocently drawn.

Taking advantage of the flood tide, which Hudson still found to be serviceable, though so far from the mouth of the river, he ran up on the nineteenth a few miles above the shoals where he had lain at anchor. Apparently the friendly Indians followed, either in their canoes or along shore, for no sooner was the *Half Moon* again at anchor than the savages were alongside with their "pompions" and various skins, besides grapes, which the earlier accounts of the Dutch settlers mention as being very plentiful throughout the country watered by the North River.

There have been reams of paper spoiled and much ink spilled in the effort to determine the precise point at which this last anchorage of the *Half Moon* was made, as it was the highest point on the river attained by Hudson. Nothing has been definitely determined except that it was in the neighbourhood of the present city of Albany. The twentieth was marked by the departure of the Dutch mate with the ship's boat and a crew of four men, to explore the river northward. The Master seems to have been inclined to sail farther in that direction, but for some reason altered his plans and sent the boat to reconnoitre instead. During the absence of the exploring party the ship's company received the savages as before, and traded with them, exchanging for valuable peltries such inconsiderable trifles as "beades, knives, and hatchets." At nightfall the boat returned. At two leagues above the anchorage the mate had found a very narrow channel with about six feet of water, but beyond that deeper water, even seven or eight fathoms.

On the twenty-first of September Hudson again resolved " yet once more to go farther up into the river, to try what depth and breadth it did bare ; but much people resorted aboard, so we went not this day."

Through some accident not recorded the fore yard of the *Half Moon* was damaged, and now the carpenter availed himself of the opportunity to go ashore and make a new stick. While this was being done Hudson and his mate conceived the idea of inviting the more important savages aboard and giving them liquor, with a view to determining " if there was any treachery in them." The excuse for this debauchery may have originated with Juet, as there seems to have been at that time no particular reason for suspecting treachery. It is more probable that the experiment of making the Indians drunk was merely a cruel practical joke.

Several chiefs, one of whom had his wife with him, were taken into the cabin of the *Half Moon* and treated to brandy and wine. They became very merry, so the account runs, except the women, " which sate so modestly as any of our countrey women would do in a strange place." Finally one old chief who had been on board constantly since the vessel anchored was very drunk, so much so that his companions became alarmed and presently went on shore, taking with them all the

savages and their canoes. In a short time the visitors
returned, bringing presents of wampum, apparently
with the idea of propitiating the spirit that had overcome their companion. "Stripes of beades" we are
told they gave him, "some had six, seven, eight, nine,
ten," but the old Indian victim to the white man's fire
water slept profoundly, oblivious to the anxiety of his
friends. In the morning, when the mate and crew had
again started with the boat upon another expedition
up-stream, the Indian awoke and found himself none
the worse for his experience. About noon his companions came aboard and were delighted at his recovery,
bringing more presents of wampum and tobacco. Not
satisfied with these attentions, some of them returned
to the shore and brought off to Hudson a "great plat-
ter of venison, dressed by themselves," and they made
him eat with them, paying him great reverence, after
which they departed, all save the old chief who had
been with them now several days and who in that short
time seems to have acquired a taste for strong drink.
In a shower of rain that night the boat returned and
the tired men reported that they had "come to an end
for shipping to go up"; in other words, had reached
the head of navigation. Eight or nine leagues they
had ascended (which, if their league was three miles,
would have given them in going and returning a journey of forty-eight miles that day), and found nothing
but shoaling water, running at last to little more than
a fathom in the channel.

The minutest details of this turning point of the trip

up the river have been set down, as far as they are
known, because they are the record of the most notable
achievement of Henry Hudson's career.   As we look
upon the 1609 voyage as one of the most important expeditions of the seventeenth century, we must consider
its culmination worthy of most minute and careful
scrutiny.

Having lain at anchor from the nineteenth to the
twenty-third of September, Hudson began to retrace
his course, weighing anchor at noon.   After going five
or six miles to a place where the channel divided, the
wind failed and a current put the *Half Moon* aground
on a shoal in the middle of the stream.   There she lay
for an hour till a little gale from the west came with
high tide and the ship slid again into deep water.   She
remained at anchor there till the following morning,
which was fair, with a favourable north-west wind blow-
ing.   The voyage was then resumed and a good run
made, bringing the navigator to the neighbourhood of
the present city of Hudson.   There the vessel grounded
again in a bed of ooze, and while waiting for the tide to
float her the crew went ashore and "gathered them a
good store of chestnuts."   At ten o'clock they came
off into deep water and anchored till the next day, which
dawned fair but with a stiff southerly gale that did not
promise favourably for the descent of the river that day;
so the greater part of the company went over to the
west shore and explored it, finding "good ground for
corn and other garden herbs, with great store of goodly
oaks, and walnut trees, and chestnut trees, ewe trees,

and trees of sweet wood (cedar?) in great abundance, and great store of slate for houses and other good stones.''

All that day and the following one the vessel remained at her anchor, for the south wind continued to blow. The carpenter, with the Dutch mate and four of the crew, went ashore to cut wood. There do not seem to have been any indications of Indian habitations at this point, but during the morning two canoes with savages in them came up the river from the point at which the *Half Moon* had lain so long on the ascent of the river, and in one of the canoes was the old man who had "lyen aboard of us at the other place." He brought another elderly savage with him, who by his gestures intimated to Hudson that he was the proprietor or chieftain of all the land thereabouts. He presented to the master great strings of wampum and showed by many signs a friendly and hospitable spirit, inviting him to visit their village two leagues farther south. Accompanying the Indians were their wives, old women, and two comely young girls ; all of whom, according to Juet, conducted themselves with the most perfect modesty and propriety. One of the old men was made happy by the gift of a knife, and at five o'clock he and his party left the *Half Moon*, making signs that the strangers should come down to them.

It happened, however, that in the morning the wind was fair, and the vessel, with foresail and maintopsail set, went past the place where the expectant savages

awaited them, to the great grief of the chief who came
alongside and begged Hudson to go ashore and feast
with him.   With a shift of the wind a little before sunset the *Half Moon* came again to an anchor, as it is
supposed, about the vicinity of Red Hook, or some
fourteen miles below Catskill Landing.   There the
boat was got out and the mate and some of the crew
went to fishing, but with indifferent luck.

The next day a run of about fifteen miles was recorded, but brought no incident worthy of note.   On
the twenty-ninth

> we weighed early in the morning, [says the jour-
> nal], and turned down three leagues by a low
> water, and anchored at the lower end of the long
> reach, for it is six leagues long.   Then there
> came certain Indians in a canoe to us, but would
> not come aboard.   After dinner there came the
> canoe with other men, whereof three came aboard
> us.   They brought Indian wheat, which we
> bought for trifles.   At three of the clock in the
> afternoon we weighed, as soon as the ebb came,
> and turned down to the edge of the mountains and
> anchored : because the high land hath many points
> and a narrow channel and hath many eddy winds.
> So we rode quietly all night in seven fathoms
> water.

A stiff gale from the Highlands came up in the morning of the last day of September.   In the face of this
wind the *Half Moon* would have made little if any
headway, so she remained at her anchor during the
forenoon and the savages came out as usual with their
canoes laden with fruit, vegetables, and skins with

which to trade for "knives and trifles." The shore of
Newburgh Bay is described as "a very pleasant place
to build a town on. The road (*i. e.* roadstead, used in
a nautical sense) is very near and very good for all
winds, save an east north-east wind."

There is a further note on the character of the nearby
shore which by its verisimilitude must impress the
reader who is familiar with the Highlands of the
Hudson. "The mountains look as if some metal or
mineral were in them. For the trees that grow on
them are all blasted, and some of them barren, with
few or no leaves on them." The hills near the upper
gate of the Highlands are to-day denuded, or almost so,
a sparse, scanty foliage only accenting the barrenness
of the outcropping ridges of metallic rock.

The record of the first of October was one of blood-
shed. It will be better to read it in Juet's own words;
the unadorned, frank, almost naïve brutality of the
journal affording a better light upon the mental pro-
cesses of seventeenth century seamen than pages of
commentary could furnish. "Fair weather, the wind
variable between the west and the north. In the
morning we weighed at seven of the clock with the
ebb, and got down below the mountains, which was
seven leagues." This brings the explorer to the
southern entrance to the Highlands, near Peekskill.

> Then it fell calm and the flood was come and
> we anchored at twelve of the clock. The people
> of the mountains came aboard us wondering at our
> ship and weapons. We bought some small skins

of them for trifles. This afternoon, one canoe kept hanging under our stern with one man in it, which we could not keep from thence, which got up by our rudder to the cabin window, and stole my pillow and two shirts and two bandaleers (leathern belts). Our master's mate shot at him and struck him in the breast; and killed him. Whereupon all the rest fled away, some in their canoes, and so leapt out of them into the water. We manned our boat and got our things again. Then one of them that swamme got hold of our boat, thinking to overthrow it. But our cook took a sword and cut off one of his hands, and he was drowned. By this time the ebb was come and we weighed and got down two leagues: by that time it was dark. So we anchored in four fathoms water and rode well.

The *second* fair weather. At break of day we weighed, the wind being at north-west, and got down seven leagues, then the flood was come strong, so we anchored. Then came one of the savages that swam away from us at our going up the river with many other, thinking to betray us. But we perceiving their intent, suffered none of them to enter our ship. Whereupon two canoes full of men, with their bows and arrows shot after our stern: in recompense whereof we discharged six muskets and killed two or three of them. Then above an hundred of them came to a point of land to shoot at us. There I shot a falcon at them, and killed two of them; whereupon the rest fled into the woods. Yet they manned off another canoe with nine or ten men, which came to meet us. So I shot at it also with a falcon, and shot it through and killed one of them. Then our men

with their muskets killed three or four more of
them.   So they went their way ; within a while
after we got down two leagues beyond that place
and anchored in a bay, clear from all danger of
them, on the other side of the river, where we saw
a very good piece of ground, and hard by it a cliff
that looked of the color of a white green, as though
it were either a copper or silver mine : and I think
it to be one of them, by the trees that grew upon
it ; for they be all burned and the other places are as
green as grass.   It is on that side of the river that
is called Manna-hata, etc.

In this account of a day's doings that were as full of
murders as one of Shakespeare's tragedies, no less than
a round dozen Indians being slain in the various
encounters, the commencement of the casualties must
have been about the neighbourhood of Stony Point and
the final anchorage in open water was in the Tappan
Zee.   Several historians, Moulton in the lead, have
been deceived by the words "on the side of the river
that is called Manna-hatta," placing the scene of the
bloody fracas near the mouth of the river, but that
view will not stand the test of analysis. Seven leagues,
we are told, took the *Half Moon* through the Highlands to the point where the first of the slaughtered
savages was caught stealing from the cabin window.
This must have been somewhere between Verplanck's
Point and the upper end of Haverstraw Bay. Two
leagues farther would bring the vessel about opposite
Teller's, or Croton, Point, and two leagues more to an
anchorage in the Tappan Zee.   The side of the river

that is called Manna-hatta, is simply a loose and ungrammatical way of saying on the same side of the river as Manna-hatta ; that is, upon the east bank.

The remainder of the voyage down the river was entirely uneventful, except for wind, rain, and "thick weather." The fourth of October

> was fair weather and the wind at north north-west. We weighed and came out of the river, into which we had run so far. Within a while after we came out also of the great mouth of the great river that runneth up to the north-west, borrowing upon the norther side of the same, thinking to have deep water ; for we had sounded a great way with our boat at our first going in, and found seven, six, and five fathoms. So we came out that way, but we were deceived, for we had but eight foot and a half water ; and so three, five, three, and two fathoms and a half. . By twelve of the clock we were clear of the inlet. Then we took in our boat and set our mainsail, and sprit sail and our topsails, and steered away east south-east, and south-east by east, off into the main sea ; and the land on the souther side of the bay or inlet did bear at noon west and by south, four leagues from us.

Van Meteren in his *Historie Der Nederlander*, after giving a synopsis of the exploration of the river by Hudson, makes the significant statement :

> When they had thus been about fifty leagues up the river, they returned on the 4th of October and went again to sea. More could have been done if the crew had been willing, and if the want of some

necessary provisions had not prevented it. While at sea they held council together, but were of different opinions. The mate, a Dutchman, advised to winter in Newfoundland, and to search the northwestern passage of Davis throughout. This was opposed by Hudson. *He was afraid of his mutinous crew, who had sometimes savagely threatened him* and he feared that during the cold season they would entirely consume their provisions and would then be obliged to return.

Although some of the crew were ill and most of them sickly, there was no talk of return to Holland, and the evident reluctance of his men on this score strengthened Hudson's suspicions. It is probable that they believed that upon reaching home the master would report their mutiny, which might have been a hanging matter ; and he, understanding this fear on their part, anticipated the execution of their threats against his life if he ventured to thwart or compel them. For this reason he therefore proposed to go to Ireland and pass the winter there, leaving the conclusion of the voyage to time and circumstances. By this move, to which the crew at once assented, Hudson insured the safety of his vessel and of his own life. It was a diplomatic compromise, not the first nor yet the least astute of the compromises upon which this remarkable voyage was accomplished.

Whether by accident or design, the *Half Moon* made Dartmouth in England, instead of the Irish coast, in a little over a month from the time of leaving the North River. From Dartmouth both captain and crew communicated with the East India Company. No other interpretation can be given to the words of Van Meteren : " *They* informed *their* employers the directors of the East India Company, etc." They proposed to the directors that they be again sent upon a voyage for a search to the north-west, and that, besides the pay, fifteen hundred florins be laid out for an additional supply of provisions. Hudson wanted six or seven of his crew exchanged for others, and the total number, then about sixteen men, raised to twenty. His plan, which seems not to have been identical with that proposed by the crew, was to leave Dartmouth on the 1st of March, so as to reach the north-western waters, where whale abounded, by the last of that month and in the neighbourhood of the Arena Islands to spend the entire spring in whale fishing, going farther into the north-west with the advance of the season and returning in the Autumn to Holland by way of the Scottish coast.

After some time the company in Amsterdam received the communications from Dartmouth, and straightway ordered the return of ship and crew to Holland. The English government, on the other hand, having learned of Hudson's arrival, forbade him or the Englishmen of his company to leave their own country, but to serve England.

Van Meteren concludes his account with these words :

Many persons thought it rather unfair that these sailors should thus be prevented from laying their accounts and reports before their employers, chiefly as the enterprise in which they had been engaged was such as to benefit navigation in general. These latter events took place in January 1610, and it was then thought probable that the English themselves would send ships to Virginia to explore the river found by Hudson.

It will be seen that Van Meteren considered that the new river was in that country which the English claimed by right of prior discovery, and named Virginia. That vague term covered all of the stretch of coast lying between New France and the Spanish possessions at the south. No Dutch writer for several years after Hudson's voyage either based any claim of territorial right upon it, or indeed thought the enterprise deserving of more than the most cursory mention. The explorer's body had long been tossed by the arctic waters in which he met his death, before the countrymen of Maurice and Olden Barneveld thought it worth while to exploit his so-called discovery in order to strengthen their own title to New Netherland.

CHAPTER IX

N the year 1610 Sir Thomas Smith, Sir Dudley Digges, and Master John Westenholm, with others of their friends, furnished out the said Henry Hudson to try if, through any of the passages which Davis saw, any passage might be found to the other ocean called the South Sea."

Such is the account written by the Rev. Samuel Purchas a few years after the fatal termination of Hudson's last voyage, and while his tragic fate was still fresh in the memories of men. His information was gathered, as ours must be, from the master's own log, from the journal written by Prickett, perhaps with a view of exculpating himself, from the chart which Hudson had made, and from the fragment of writing found in the desk of Thomas Wydowse, one of the party who suffered by the final act of the mutineers. Out of such material it is possible to construct a consecutive narrative of the voyage; which in all its essential features may be relied upon.

The seventeenth of Aprill, 1610, we brake ground
and went downe from Saint Katherine's poole
and fell down to Blackwall, and so plied down
with the ships to Lee, which was the two and
twentieth day.

This is Hudson's own account of the beginning of
his fourth voyage and it furnishes at least one ground
for conjecture. What does the navigator mean by
" the ships ? " Is it merely a reference to the vessels
that waited in the Thames for a favourable tide, and
slipped down to Blackwall in company with the
little *Discoverer;* or are we to understand that
Hudson started out with a small fleet under his
command, as he may perhaps have done upon his
third voyage? It is certain that neither upon the
third nor fourth voyages do we learn of more than
one vessel that proceeded far beyond the starting
point.

Our navigator's crew seems upon this as upon other
occasions to have been poorly chosen. He took with
him, in an ill defined position and apparently from
purely philanthropic motives, a dissolute fellow
named Henry Greene, whom his own people had
cast off as incorrigible. This neer-do-weel Hudson
had harboured in his own house in London, when
because of his vices Greene was an outcast from his
own people. He had appealed in his behalf to an
obdurate family, and finally took him upon a des-
perate voyage in the hope of reforming, or at least
of keeping him out of mischief. Hudson's relations

with Greene would alone furnish material for a
romance or a tragedy.

Colebert, or Coolbrand, was another objectionable
member of Hudson's crew. He was detected by the
master in some dereliction before the *Discoverer* was
fairly out of sight of the smoke of London, and was
shipped back at the first opportunity. We know
neither this man's offence nor his subsequent fate, but
he was evidently the subject of some controversy at the
time. Captain Luke Fox, in his brief comment upon
Hudson's last voyage, gave the following version of
the discharge of Coolbrand.

> In the road of Lee, in the river Thames, he
> caused Master Coolbrand to be set in a pinke to be
> carried back again to London. This Coolbrand
> was in every way a better man than himselfe *being
> put in by the adventurers as his assistant*, who envy-
> ing the same (he having the command in his own
> hand) devised this course to send himselfe in the
> same way, though in a far worse course, as here-
> after followeth.

The interpretation of this intemperate fling at the
memory of the man whose death aroused the pity and
indignation of all England, seems to be that Coolbrand
was sent out as Hudson's mate, but that the master,
through jealousy, seized the earliest opportunity to get
rid of him. The testimony is altogether too slight and
the probabilities insufficient to warrant us in drawing
such a conclusion.

If there was an evil genius thwarting Hudson's ambition and turning to naught his cherished plans and

bravest efforts, that genius was Greene, the outcast, the reprobate, the beneficiary. In Hudson's own words the discharge of Coolbrand—mate or mariner— takes a different complexion. "The two and twentieth I caused Master Coleburne to bee put into a pinke bound for London, with my letter to the adventurers, importing the reason wherefore I so put him out of the ship, and so plyed forth."

It is evident from further happenings recorded by Prickett that our old acquaintance Robert Juet was chosen as the Master's Mate. More and more is our curiosity aroused to discover what anomolous position this elderly man (for so we are told he was) held in relation to Hudson's life. That he was more than a common sailor is evident, that his fortunes and those of the navigator were intimately connected cannot be doubted ; yet in a little while we shall find him dealing treacherously with his chief, and deposed, as Coolbrand had been, to be succeeded in his turn by Robert Billet.

By the second of May Hudson was "thwart of" Flamborough Head, on the Yorkshire coast, and on the fifth made the Orkney Islands, where in his own words, "I set the north end of the needle and the end of the flie all one." If we may suppose "flie" in this connection to refer to his vessel, a *vlie* or flie-boat, as the *Half Moon* was, then we will read that the course from the Orkneys was due north. The explorer makes note of the fact that he found by observation that the north end of Scotland, Orkney, and the Shetland Islands, was not as far north as generally set down by geographers of his day.

Hudson mentions sailing within sight of the Faroe Islands and the Westmania group, that belongs to Iceland ; but gives none of the details of a delay upon the coast of Iceland, enforced by contrary winds for fifteen days. For these we must look to the journal of Prickett, and a letter of Thomas Wydhouse. At

> Westmonie [we are told], the king of Denmark hath a fortresse, by which we passed to rayse Snow Hill foot, a mountain so called on the northwest part of the land. But in our course we saw that famous hill, Mount Hecla, which cast out much fire　　　　 Wee leave Island (Iceland) astern of us, and met a mayne of ice, which did hang on the north part of Island, and stretched downe to the west, which when our Master saw, he stood back for Island to find an harbour, which we did on the Northwest part, called Derefer (Dyre-fiord) where we killed good store of fowle. From thence we put to sea again, but neither wind nor weather serving, our master stood back for this harbour again, but could not reach it, but fell in with another to the south of that, called by our Englismen Lousie Bay: where on the shoare wee found an hot bath, and here all our Englishmen bathed themselves.

There is in this repetition of "our Englishmen" a suggestion that Hudson was again afloat with a mixed crew, of which only part were his own countrymen. We are obliged to the narrator for his testimony to their cleanliness. Thomas Wydhouse, one of Hudson's

company, wrote from Iceland upon the thirtieth of May
to his friend Master Samuel Macham :

> Master Macham, I heartily commend me to you
> etc.   I can write unto you no newes, though I
> have seene much, but such as every English fisher-
> man haunting these coasts can report better than
> myselfe.
>
> We kept our Whitsunday in the northeast coast
> of Island (Iceland), and I think I never fared
> better in England than we feasted there.   They of
> the country are very poore and live miserably,
> yet we found therein store of fresh fish and daintie
> fowle.   I myselfe in an afternoon killed so many
> fowle as feasted all our company, being three and
> twenty persons, at one time, onely with partridges,
> besides curlew, plover, Mallard, teale and goose.
> I have seene two hot baths in Island and have
> beene in one of them.   Wee are resolved to try to
> the uttermost and lye onely expecting a faire wind,
> and to refresh ourselves to avoid the ice, which
> now is come off the west coasts, of which we have
> seen whole islands but God be thanked, have not
> been in danger of any.   Thus I desire all your
> prayers for us.

On the first day of June a final successful start was
made for Greenland, which was " raysed " on the fourth,
one day having been consumed in a vain chase after
a new island which proved in the end to be nothing
more than a fog bank.   The coast of Greenland was so
encumbered by ice that a near approach was impossible, though the land could be plainly seen.   In four
days more our navigator records that he was off Frobisher's Strait " with the winde northerly, and plyed

unto the south westward untill the fifteenth day
we were in sight of land in latitude 59 degrees, 27 minutes, which was called by captayne John Davis Desolation, and found the errour of the former laying down
of that land."

In explanation of the foregoing extract it should
be understood that the geographers of Hudson's day
had delineated Frobisher's Strait in Greenland, or
rather as separating the southern end of Greenland,
which they called Desolation, from the northern part,
which they named Groneland or Groenland.

By the fifth of July the *Discoverer* was battling with
the ice upon the southern extremity of " Desolation "
and after three days Hudson discovered "land from
the northwest by west, half northerly, unto the south-
west by west, covered with snow, a champaigne land,
and called it Desire Provoketh." This is without
question the record or the explorer's first sight of
the Labrador coast. Without himself comprehending
his position he penetrated for some distance into the
mouth of the great strait which now bears his name,
anchored thankfully near three rocky islands which he
called the " Isles of God's mercy "—since identified as
the Saddle Back group, to the south of Jackman's
Sound—and noted a tide-rise of something more than
twenty-four feet. At this point Prickett records that
he was sent ashore with a party, starting a covey
of partridge and shooting "the old one." On the
nineteenth Hudson was in Ungava Bay near a shore
which he named " Hold with Hope." " Here," he

wrote, "I found the sea more growne than any wee had since wee left England."

Among the fields of ice he made his way slowly westward, plying to and fro, northward or southward as circumstances permitted, but always toward the west, and the great bay where he should end his career. Strange islands were discovered and explored and names as strange were bestowed upon them ; Prince Henry's Foreland, King James his Cape, etc.

Upon a foggy morning the vessel was driven by the tide far into an inlet flowing from the north-west ; and the depth of this water, together with "the playing forward of the ice," at once roused in Hudson the hope that it would prove the passage he had so long sought. Again and again had he cherished a similar expectation only to find it ending in disappointment, but no failure, no dashing of his expectations, could quell his natural optimism. It was once said by Washington Irving that at a certain time in his life Oliver Goldsmith "lost his faculty of hoping." It seems certain that until the very last scene of his life Hudson did not lose that faculty. It buoyed him up through disappointment after disappointment and afforded him solace in defeat.

After sailing in the strait he had found to a distance which he computed to be three hundred leagues west, he came to another inlet or tributary of the first. Into this channel he penetrated for more than six miles, finding the water very deep. At the farther end were two headlands which because of their height seemed much nearer together than was actually the case. The point upon the south Hudson named Cape Westenholm, and that upon the north-west Digges' Island. To explore the latter and to see from the high land what lay beyond it, Prickett with the carpenter and several others were sent ashore. "We had further to it than we thought," comments Prickett, "for the land is very high, and we were overtaken with a storm of rain, thunder and lightning." Because of the steepness of the cliffs no landing was possible upon the east side of the land, but towards the south-west the character of the shore was less rugged and there they succeeded in disembarking. Deer were seen but not near enough to be brought down by their rude muskets. A great waterfall "that would have turned an overshot mill," grass that was a reminder of that grown in England, immense flocks of wild fowl, and other noteworthy features are duly recorded by the observant Prickett. Most curious of all were groups of mounds or cairns of stone, which at first the Englishmen took to be grass-cocks, but which upon examination proved to be "hollow within, and full of fowles hanged by their neckes."

After an exploration to no particular purpose beyond what has been recounted, the men were recalled to the vessel by the firing of guns. They described the pleasantness of the land they had seen and begged Hudson to tarry there several days "telling him what refreshing might there be had." He, however, was obdurate in his refusal, "so," as Prickett ruefully concludes, "we left the fowle and lost our way down to the south west."

The points at which Hudson approached the shore line on the east side of the great bay, after leaving Cape Westenholm astern, cannot possibly be determined. He was at last in a spacious sea, and his heart bounded with hope because he was confident that he had traversed the passage and was *en route* for the Indies. It may well be that the discovery of his error broke his heart. After a hundred leagues he found himself in a bay and was obliged to turn again towards the north. It may have been that this disappointment had its effect upon the tempers both of the master and his crew. Some time before, upon being caught in the ice field near Iceland, Robert Juet and others had expressed great dissatisfaction, yet the master at that time overlooked their fault. Now as Juet himself seems to have been bent upon adding new fuel to the old fire, and for the second time openly criticised the conduct of his superior, Hudson "took occasion to revive old matters, and to displace Robert Juet from being his mate, and the boatswaine from his place, for the words spoken upon the first great bay of ice.

From a note subsequently found in the desk of Wydhouse may be obtained a full and very clear impression of the true cause and extent of the breach between Hudson and his mate. It is worth quoting verbatim ; only modernising the spelling.

> The tenth day of September 1610, after dinner, our master called all the company together, to hear

and bear witness of the abuse of some of the company; it having been the request of Robert Juet that the master should redress some abuses and slanders, as he called them against this Juet; which thing after the Master had examined and heard with equity what he could say for himself, they were proved so many and great abuses, and mutinous matters against the master, and action by Juet, that there was danger to have suffered them longer; and it was fit time to punish and cut off farther occasions of like mutinies.

In reading the foregoing paragraph it should be noted that by the word " action " Wydhouse refers to the voyage, otherwise the enterprise or action in which they were engaged.

It was proved to his (Juet's) face, first with Bennet Mathew, our trumpet (?) upon our first sight of Iceland, and he confessed that he supposed the action would be manslaughter, and prove bloody to some.

Secondly, at our coming from Iceland, in hearing of the company he did threaten to turn the head of the ship home from the action, which at that time was by our master wisely pacified, hoping of amendment.

Thirdly, it was deposed by Philip Staffe our carpenter, and Ladlie Arnold, to his face upon the holy bible, that he persuaded them to keep muskets charged and swords ready in their cabins, for they should be charged with shot ere the voyage was over.

Fourthly, we being pestered in the ice, he had used words tending to mutiny, discouragement and slander of the action, which easily took effect on them that were timorous; and had not the master prevented, it might easily have overthrown the voyage. And now lately, being embayed in a deep bay, which the master had desire to see, for some reason to himself known, his word tended altogether to put the company into a fray of extremity, by wintering in cold. Jesting at our Master's hope to see Bantam by Candlemas.

For these and divers other base slanders against the Master he was deposed, and Robert Bylot, who had showed himself honestly respecting the good of the action, was placed in his stead the Master's mate.

Also Francis Clement, the boatswain, at this time was put from his office, and William Wilson, a man thought more fit, preferred to his place. This man had basely carried himself to our master and to the action.

Also Adrian Mooter was appointed boatswain's mate, and a promise by the master that from this day Juet's wages should remain to Bylot, and the boatswain's overplus of wages should be equally divided between Wilson and one John King to the owner's good liking, one of the quartermasters, who had very well carried themselves to the furtherance of the business.

Also the master promised, if the offenders yet behaved themselves henceforth honestly, he would be a means of their good and that he would forget injuries, with other admonitions.

These details are more explicit than any given by Prickett but wherever the two accounts touch upon the same matter they are found to agree as to facts and names.

The *Discoverer* now plied in thick and foul weather from north to south and then back again from south to north, making little progress, frequently embayed, hampered by ice and fog. Just where she sailed we have no means of discovering, but there seems little doubt that for a time Hudson was lost in one of those tedious clusters of nameless islands that pepper the eastern shore of Hudson Bay. Finally the vessel was brought to an anchor in a shoal bay, and there lay eight days at the mercy of the elements. Then Hudson resolved to weigh and continue the voyage in spite of the weather and the remonstrances of his crew. Prickett's account is graphic :

> Well, to it we went, and when we had brought it (the anchor) to a peake, a sea tooke her and cast us all off from the capstone, and hurt divers of us. Heere we lost our anchor and if the carpenter had not beene, we had lost our cable too ; but he (fearing such a matter) was ready with an axe and so cut it.

The chronicler says that Hudson took up the anchor " against the mind of all who knew what belonged thereto."

To the southward once more they stood, coming into a sea of divers colours and soundings. When the night came they took in topsails and ran before the wind with fore and mainsails set, till in the darkness they discovered that the water had shoaled to six fathoms ; when they sailed to the eastward till they found deep water again. Feeling their way once more to the south and west they finally ran into what some commentators believe to be the most south-westerly pocket of James Bay, that is to say the very southernmost point of Hudsons Bay, not more than three hundred miles as the crow flies, across what is now Ontario to Lake Superior.

A boat was sent out to the nearest shore, but near the land the water was too shoal to float her, so the crew were obliged to wade. Upon the snowy rocks they found the footprints of a man, the first indication of human life, except the cairns upon Digges Island, that they had encountered since leaving Iceland.

At midnight the *Discoverer* was again under way and trying to get out of the bay by the course she followed when she came in. The carpenter upon this sought Hudson and advised him that he would send the vessel upon the rocks, but he was confident that he was far enough out to clear them, till presently they were hard and fast and lay in that perilous position twelve hours. The vessel was scarred, though not badly injured, but the prestige of the master suffered by this and other mishaps and the mutinous spirit of discontent was steadily gaining headway among the crew. Juet was already alienated, as was also the boatswain, a serious defection in so small a company, and now others were coming to their standard. History gives us few examples of leaders whose popularity and power have grown in spite of repeated defeat, the most notable example being that of Washington. Hudson was not one of the few chosen leaders whose personality outweighs all the circumstances of

their lot, and inspires loyalty even in the face of
disaster.

After many toilsome weeks of fruitless endeavour,
when October had come and nearly passed, Hudson
ordered his carpenter and Prickett ashore to select a
place in which to winter. On the first of November
the ship was brought to a bay or inlet far down into
the south-west, and hauled aground ; and there by the
tenth of the month she was frozen in. Discontent was
no longer expressed in whispers. The men were aware
that the provisions, laid in for a limited number of
months, were running to an end, and they murmured
that they had not been taken back for winter quarters
to Digges' Island, where such stores of wild fowl had
been seen, instead of beating about for months in "a
labyrinth without end."

Hudson now made rules for the apportionment of the
provisions on hand, or in other words put the crew
upon a limited allowance, but at the same time offered
rewards for whatever game should be secured to aug-
ment the slender supply. Billet, the mate, was one of
the most expert hunters, as he seems to have been
efficient in other respects.

It was a fortunate circumstance and indeed a chief
factor in the salvation of the crew, that birds visited
them in great numbers. Of the white ptarmigan or
partridge we are told that they killed about a hundred
and twenty dozen. These were to them what the quail
were to the Israelites in the desert, sustaining both life
and courage. In December the surgeon, a Hollander,

applied a decoction made from the leaves of a tree, to
the various ills to which sailors in cold latitudes are
subject. This tree we are told blossomed in the cold
weather, with leaves green and yellow,

> and being boiled yielded an oily substance which
> proved excellent salve, and the decoction being
> drunk proved as wholesome a potion, whereby
> they were cured of the scorbute, sciaticus, cramps,
> convultions, and other diseases which the coldness
> of the climate bred in them.

In the depth of the winter, when the hardship of
their situation was at its height, an open rupture between Hudson and one of his most important subordinates occurred. This was John King, the carpenter,
an illiterate but apparently not unintelligent man.
Hudson ordered him to build on shore a house that
should serve them for a shelter, and the carpenter refused, surlily adding that the snow and frost were too
heavy to permit such work. The master was angry
—perhaps excusably so—and hauled King out of his
quarters, threatening " with many foule names," according to Prickett, to hang him. The carpenter, sub-
mitting finally to a show of force, did build the house,
though he averred that he was a ship carpenter and no
house carpenter; that he " knew his place better than
the captain did," etc.

Following shortly upon this altercation came another.
John Williams, the gunner, died, and it was murmured that Hudson had treated him badly. No sooner
had he been buried than the men claimed that according to custom his belongings should be brought to the

mainmast and there auctioned. Among the dead man's effects was a grey cloth gown or coat that Greene asked for, claiming that the master had promised it to him ; but before he received it, he went ashore with the carpenter, who was then out of favour, and so incurred the displeasure of his chief. The result was that Billet, the mate, got the gown, and when Greene angrily reminded Hudson of his promise the latter opened the vials of his wrath and reproached his ungrateful protégé with the many things he knew to his discredit. It was a pitiful situation ; the strong man, worn out by anxiety, responsibility, hope deferred, and mistrust of those around him, finally yielded to very human anger and added another to the growing circle of his enemies.

> You shall see, [adds the voluble Prickett], how the devil out of this so wrought with Greene, that he did the master what mischief he could in seeking to discredit him, and to thrust him and many honest men out of the ship in the end.

It is lamentable that we have only Prickett's version of this and other troubles of that dark winter and spring. It is inexplicable and not forgivable that Samuel Purchas, having Hudson's own account at hand, "omitted for brevity" any of it.

With the coming of spring the ptarmigan were succeeded by other birds ; "swan, goose, teal, duck ; all easy to take." There came also abundant schools of all manner of fish, and Hudson ordered that both these and the birds should be taken and cured to supply their

depleted stores.   But unhappily, with the open weather
the explorer's dream of finding the passage returned,
and he exhausted the greater part of what provisions
were left while examining the western shore of the
bay.   The restocking of the larder was left to incom-
petent or careless hands, and before long starvation
was imminent.   Then the men went into the valleys of
the hills and dug roots, caught frogs and ate them,
and subsisted on "mosse of the grounde, than the
which I take the powder of a post to bee much better."

There is but one record of meeting with any savages
on that shore.   One of the natives visited certain
members of the crew—probably while they were searching for food—and was presented with a knife and some
bits of glass, with which he was much delighted, returning with a sled laden with beavers and deer skins.

While the fish were running, before the days of extreme famine, Greene and Wilson, who were of the
fishing party detailed to secure a supply for the vessel,
conspired to run away with the net and shallop, and
shift for themselves; but this plan was frustrated by
the master's setting forth upon the exploration above
referred to.   On his return from that expedition he
made ready to abandon the search and sail homeward.   The bread in the bread room came to a pound
apiece for each man's share, and this he delivered to
them.   He "delivered also a bill of returne, willing
then to have that to shew, if it pleased God that they
came home ; and he wept when he gave it to them."
A few small fish, fourscore in all, were added to the

provision doled out, and then the capstan was manned, the anchor came aboard, and the *Discoverer* moved out of the little basin where she had wintered. Hudson now distributed the last of the cheeses, nine in all. Some of the men were economical, striving to make their meagre provisions last as long as possible; others —Greene and Wilson particularly—devoured all that they had in a few hours and were ill. Some of the more temperate among the company remonstrated with Hudson for putting all of the ship's small stock of cheese at once into the hands of the men, pointing out that the more improvident would soon be in want, as we have seen was really the case. The master's answer to this objection was reasonable : the food, particularly the cheeses, was not all in the same condition, some part of the provinder being nearly spoiled. By distributing at once, share and share alike, he hoped to avoid any imputation of unfairness. Then, as soon as the more greedy had exhausted their portion, they raised another cry, that some of the food had been kept back. There were several cheeses, they insisted, that were not accounted for.

With a fair wind, in the month of June, Hudson commenced his return voyage. On the eighteenth of that month the *Discoverer* was stopped by ice and then the discontent among the men again gathered head. Billet, in his turn had been deposed, and King, the carpenter, who could neither read nor write, was elevated to his place. The anger of the master against this man seems to have been short lived, and in the end the carpenter proved to be more worthy of confidence than most of his companions.

By what at this distance seems a serious error of judgment Hudson still further widened the deplorable breach between himself and his men by such a drastic exercise of authority as would not be resorted to except under conditions of extreme necessity. He ordered Nicholas Simmes to break open the sea-chests of the men and collect whatever food might be concealed, to be redistributed. This was done and as the result a bag containing thirty cakes was brought by Simmes to the master. Open mutiny followed so close upon this act that we cannot escape the conviction that it was one of the immediate causes of the outbreak.

On the night of Saturday, the twenty-first of June, one year from the time that the *Discoverer* had encountered the heavy seas in Ungava Bay, Prickett was lying lame in his bunk, when Henry Greene came to him secretly, with Wilson, the boatswain, and whispered such a plan of treachery as must have provoked instant opposition from a man who was both honest and brave. Which of these qualities Prickett lacked, or whether he possessed either of them, we do not know. Pious he was, after a puritanical fashion, as we gather from his journal, which is full of religious phrases and scripture quotations. Both honest and brave his own words prove him not to have been.

Greene told the lame man that he and his associates were resolved to seize the ship, take the command into their own hands, and turn the master and the sick members of the crew adrift in a shallop.

Prickett avers that he remonstrated with these conspirators, and there is no testimony to contradict his ; but his opposition was certainly not strenuous.

> When I heard this [he says], I told them I marvelled to hear so much from them, considering that they were married men, and had wives and children, and that for their sakes they should not commit so foule a thing in the sight of God and man as that would bee; for why should they banish themselves from their native countrie?

Greene scoffed at this objection ; said that the worst that could happen to them was hanging, and for his part he would rather be hanged at home than starved abroad. There were not, he pointed out, fourteen days' rations left on board, even doled out as the provision had been. He declared that Hudson did not care to go one way or the other. He was resolute, being hungry.

The plotters told Prickett that they entertained such a feeling of good will toward him that they intended to allow him to remain on the ship. He answered that he had not entered her with any intention of quitting, but that nevertheless he would not hold with any such wickedness. Greene retorted that in that case he must take his fate in the shallop.

" The will of God be done," piously responded Prickett.

It was not the will of God, certainly not the will of Prickett, that he should go in the shallop. Greene went off storming and vowing to kill any one who crossed him, and Wilson remained to argue with the scribe. The latter begged for three days' time, during which he pledged himself to influence Hudson to do whatever they wished. No? then two days—twelve hours, at least.

Greene returned and again insisted upon carrying out his hateful plan. He said that if they did not strike while the iron was hot some of the crew would be swerved from their purpose. Upon being told that it appeared to be revenge and not justice that he was seeking, he took up Prickett's Bible and swore roundly upon the book that he would do no man harm ; that it was for the good of the voyage and nothing else that he acted, and that the crew were with him. Wilson followed the example of his leader.

While this was going on Robert Juet, the former mate, came in. Prickett tried to reason with, or at least to sound him, and hoped "because he was an ancient man, to have found some reason in him," but he was worse than Greene and "swore that he would justify this deed when he got home." John Thomas and Michael Perce followed, then Moter and Bennett. The last two took oath as Greene and Wilson had done.

It was a scene such as has been enacted in many a forecastle ; an angry group of malcontents, hungry and undisciplined ; an atmosphere of tobacco smoke, train oil, and humanity that itself might be enough to incite to crime ; an evil smelling apology for a lamp, adding its increment to the sickening effluvia; a conversation carried on in undertones and garnished with strange oaths, with intent to convince or silence some coward who dared not either refuse or accede to the general devilment. Prickett was a Puritan, a man with a conscience. He found it necessary to silence either Greene and his companions, or that conscience. With some difficulty and no little assistance he succeeded in accomplishing the latter feat.

He planned or composed a form of oath which he insisted upon their subscribing to, as indeed they did readily. "You shall swear truth to God, your prince, and countrie; you shall do nothing, but to the glory of God and the good of the action in hand, and harme to noe man." The author of this beautiful and noncommittal piece of pedantry then called Greene and begged that nothing be done till morning.

Hudson did not rest that night. In his cabin until daylight Greene kept him company. Once the cabinboy gave the conspirators some bread which the latter conveyed to Prickett. All of those in the plot were watchful, no man trusting his neighbour. Prickett got an opportunity to ask Greene who were to be put in the boat with Hudson, and the answer was prompt—all the sick men, and John King. King, with whom Greene was lately intimate, whose own outbreak of insubordination had only a short time before been met by a threat of hanging, was now in favour with the master and consequently hated by the crew. He was the mate, and they complained that Hudson had made him so because he could neither read nor write, and therefore could not interfere with the navigation of the vessel.

Let us take Prickett's account of the position of the men at this time.

> To begin in the cooke roome: There lay Bennet and the cooper, lame ; without the cooke roome, on the steere-board side, lay Thomas Wydhouse, sicke ; next to him lay Sydrack Funer,lame ; then the surgeon and John Hudson with him ; next to them lay Wilson the boatswaine, and then Arnold Lodlo next to him ; in the gun room lay Robert Juet and John Thomas ; on the larboord side lay Michael Bute and Adria Moore, who had never been well since we lost our anchor ; next to them lay Michael Perce and Andrew Moter. Next to them, without the gun room lay John King and with him Robert Billet ; next to them myself and next to me Francis Clements. In the midships, betweene the capstone and the pumpes, lay Henrie Greene and Nicholas Simmes."

King was up late and was thought to be with the master, but apprehensions were relieved when it was discovered that he had been with the new carpenter. As he came to the hatch Billet met him as though by accident and went with him to the cabin. No one slept ; every man was spying upon his neighbour and fearing the exposure of their plans.

Bennet—who seems to have been the cook—in the early morning came to the water butts to get water for his kettle. At that moment King went into the hold and immediately some one closed and held the hatch.

At this Bennet sprang towards the deck, with John Thomas and Wilson close behind him.

Hudson now came out of his cabin. Grave and worn by months of hardship and anxiety, he was still the master, refusing to comprehend that those over whom he had lately exercised command were at that instant in rebellion against his authority. Thomas and Bennet confronted him, and no doubt his brow lowered and his eyes burned as a rebuke at their insolent manner sprang to his lips: but before he could utter that rebuke Wilson seized him from behind and bound his arms.

"What does this mean?" he cried.

"You will know fast enough when you are in the shallop"; was the sinister answer.

In the meantime King, in the hold, was making what resistance he could. Juet went down to secure him, but the ex-carpenter had a sword, and showed such an evident inclination to use it that "the ancient man" cried for help. Several of his fellows came running to him and after a struggle succeeded in tying their victim and bringing him to the deck. Hudson is said to have called to the carpenter "They have bound me." No reply has been recorded, but Bute and Lodlo railed at them and said scurrilous things, barking as such curs must at such a time.

In great haste the conspirators got the shallop to the ship's side and all the sick and lame were ordered to get out of their bunks and were lowered into the boat. Hudson, before they put him over the side, called for

Prickett, who managed to get to the companionway and so to the deck, and besought the mutineers to think better of what they were doing ; but they curtly ordered him to go back to his bed, and he obeyed. When the master was in the shallop his face was on a level with the horn covered deadlight on the other side of which was Prickett's quarters.

"Juet has done this," said the master.   "He will overthrow ye all."

"No !" called the scribe (we have his word for it that he spoke not softly).   "It is that villain Greene."

A man of different make from Prickett was the new carpenter, Philip Staffe, King's successor, who was no scribe, but a true-hearted Englishman after all.   Not choosing to lose his skill they gave him his liberty, but he told them they were a pack of thieves who would all be hanged when they got home.   For his part he would not stay on the ship unless he was held there by force.   So the carpenter in turn went into the shallop, going of his own will, as far as is known the only one not bound, possibly as ignorant as any man of the crew, but above them all in courage, honour, and loyalty.   By some freak of generosity, or perhaps because his manliness had touched even their hardness and meanness the new masters of the *Discoverer* let him have his chest of tools, which he demanded, and it was lowered into the boat after him.

John Hudson, generally supposed to have been the master's son, though there is no absolute proof of their relationship, was also put in the shallop.

There was a dispute over two of the sick men, Francis Clement and the cooper. Thomas was the friend of one and Bennet of the other, and they declared that these men should not be sent adrift with Hudson and his enfeebled companions. Greene violently demanded that they be put over the side, and presently there was a party formed, when a resolute man, had he been there, might have made a diversion that would have saved the prisoners. But the moment passed: Clement and his companion indeed were saved, but the remainder of the sick were hurried into the boat and the lines that held her being cut she drifted astern.

During all of this scene the only record that we have gives no indication that the master condescended to ask for his life or that he exhibited any sign of rage or despair. On the contrary, we have a glimpse of a figure whose calmness and poise were in strong contrast to the confusion about him. It was a heroic figure, even in adversity. As the icy distance between the ship and the shallop slowly increased the conspirators put on sail to get away from it. A sort of panic seized them to escape from that calm, self-controlled man, that sat among his miserable companions, unconquered.

Hours afterwards there was a rumour that the shallop was in sight again. "They let fall the mainsayle," we are told, " out with their top sayles, and fly as from an enemy."

The names of those who were set adrift with Hudson in the cold expanse of Hudson's Bay have been preserved. They are John Hudson, Arnold Lodlo, Sidrach Faner, Phillip Staffe, Thomas Wydhouse, Adam Moore, Henrie (?) King, Michael Bute. They had aboard a gun, some powder and shot, an iron pot, the carpenter's chest, some meal, and a few other things.

No sooner was Hudson away than his late company ransacked and pillaged the *Discoverer* from stem to stern. Chests and drawers were broken open and emptied of their contents, the goods of the poor fellows in the shallop were taken by those who had been their messmates, and the cabin was rifled of whatever attracted the fancy of the robbers. Prickett claims that "we" found in the master's cabin two hundred biscuit cakes, a quantity of meal and a butt of beer. When the hold was examined the list of its contents was as follows: Of two vessels of meal with which they started one was unbroken and the other only partly used; there were two firkins of butter, twenty-seven pieces of pork, and half a bushel of peas. This was all the provision that could be found for a dozen or more men, against a long and perilous voyage.

We have no knowledge of the locality in which the tragedy just described took place, except that we have a vague assurance that it was somewhere on the eastern side of the great bay that we now call Hudson's. The position of the first land made by the *Discoverer* after the mutiny is equally uncertain. Somewhere upon that eastern shore they found an island, and anchored in sixteen or seventeen fathoms of water. From this anchorage the boat and net were dispatched to the shore to endeavour to get a haul of fish. Failing in this effort, because of the rocks, Perce landed with his gun and shot two birds with which he returned to the ship.

Prickett was now summoned by Greene, so he says, to take up his quarters in the master's cabin. " I told him," said the scribe, " that it was more fit for Robert Juet; he said he should not come in it nor meddle with the master's cards (charts) nor journals. So up I came, and Henrie Greene gave me the key of the master's chest, and told me then, that he had laid the master's best things together, which he would use himselfe when time did serve. The bread also was delivered to me by tale."

Certainly this was a much more comfortable situation for a reflective man than the bare thwart of an open boat on a stormy and icy sea. The scribe had chosen more wisely than the carpenter.

Billet and Juet seemed to divide the duties of navigating officer between them at the outset. The former evidently had the greater authority in this department, though in the general command the dissolute Greene was chief. The treatment accorded to Prickett merits some explanation. Purchas believed that the writer of the journal was spared because as a man of education and possibly of some influence, he might plead for his guilty companions when they arrived at home. It is perhaps not singular that Prickett's severest animadversions are for those who did not return. He was put in Hudson's cabin that he might have access to the papers, journals, and charts that were there and with every advantage prepare his brief which might save Greene and company from the gallows. Still another reason there may have been for putting the journalist in the room of the man they had turned adrift to die. Sailors of that period, as of this, were superstitious, and they who had crowded sail to escape from the fancied pursuit of the shallop after she had been left out of sight on the stormy sea, would be loth to risk facing the master's ghost.

It is a coincidence so singular that I cannot forbear to notice it that while this chapter is being written, three centuries, lacking less than three years, after the last futile effort of Hudson to find the north-west passage, another man of another nationality has achieved the first successful voyage through the long sought, long doubted waterway that bounds the northern limit of the American continent. In the diminutive sloop *Gjoa* of less than fifty tons burden, a brave and able Norwegian has accomplished that feat that to explorers and geographers has ranked only second to the discovery of the geographical North Pole. The world is calmer now than in the days when Hudson made his daring ventures. We are told that there is little left upon the globe to discover : that the prizes, all save the capital one for which Peary has been the latest contestant, have been awarded. Nevertheless, we pay honour to Captain Roald Amundsen, who has succeeded where Davis and Frobisher, where Ross and Baffin, failed ; and where Hudson and Franklin perished ; and as we uncover to him let us not forget his prototype, who sailed in the employ of Sir Dudley Digges and his associates, and whose soul is sailing on.

Of Hudson's own chart of his fourth voyage, brought home by the mutineers, sent to Peter Plantius in Amsterdam and engraved and published with Latin notes in repeated editions by Hessel Gerritz, Dr. G. M. Asher makes the following remarkable statement : '' The deliniation may seem a poor work to modern eyes, but when we apply the standards of Hudson's time instead of our own, we find this chart to be far superior to many contemporary productions and decidedly *facile princeps* of all the then existing deliniations of the arctic regions.''

A word may be added to the foregoing narrative as a sop to the modern fetich which editors are wont to call '' timeliness.'' Within the year the report of the Canadian Geological Survey has been issued and it deals principally with the present conditions of Hudson's Bay and the Canadian Arctic Islands. The Hon. A. P. Low, in charge of the expedition upon which the report is based, was intent upon securing data concerning the geology, botany, natural history, etc., of the shores of the great bay, but particularly in collecting all possible information relating to the navigability of that tract of water over which the dominion of Canada has recently been formally asserted.

The gist of Mr. Low's report, after an exhaustive recapitulation of historic facts regarding former explorations, and a careful summary of statements concerning present conditions, is that in order to make the shores of the bay commercially available, and ordinary navigation upon its waters practicable, all that is necessary is a line of railroad communication to one of its southern ports.

CHAPTER X

"THE wind serving wee stood to the north-east, and this was Robert Billet's course, contrarie to Robert Juet, who woulde have gone to the north-west."

So commences the story of the return voyage of the *Discoverer*. Already the discord to be expected among men of such unstable character had begun to develop. Billet's course, after they were free from the ice, took the vessel into the neighbourhood of several groups of small islands, near the mouth of Mosquito Bay. Here they searched with little success for food, finding only some " cockle grass," of which they brought aboard a store. One of the clusters was recognised as having been discovered upon the outward voyage. Hudson had named it Rumney's Islands.

"Between these and the shallow ground," writes Prickett, "our master went down into the first great bay. We kept the east shore still in sight—after leaving Rumney's Island astern—and coming thwart of the low land wee ranne on a rocke that lay under water, and strooke but once ; for if she had, we might have been made inhabitants of that place; but God sent us soone off without any harm that wee saw."

Soon there was an outcry against Billet. His companions declared that his northerly course had caused them to overrun the mouth of the passage and that they must turn at once and go southward, for their stock of provisions was nearly spent. Billet answered that he was as likely to find means to relieve their hunger going north as south, so he continued to sail in the same direction. Then Prickett sided with Billet, telling his companions that the land they saw to the east of them, stretching northward, was the mainland below Westenholm Cape. This opinion proved correct and ere long the forlorn company rejoiced to see Digges' Island, where they had upon their previous visit found such abundance of wild fowl.

Upon reaching this long-looked-for haven they discovered that it was inhabited by savages, who were at first exceedingly friendly and showed them how to snare the wild fowl, which were as numerous as before. But suddenly, when all suspicion of treachery had been allayed, either because of anger at some unrecorded act of the white man, or because of a desire to possess their boat, the savages made a sudden attack upon them.

Prickett's account of the trouble is as follows:

When we came (upon the second visit to the shore) they made signs to their dogges—whereof there were many like mongrels, as bigge as hounds —and pointed to their mountaine and to the sunne, clapping their hands. Then Henry Greene, John

Thomas, and William Wilson stood hard by the
boate head, Michael Perse and Andrew Moter
were got up upon a rock a gathering of sorrell ; not
one of them had any weapon about him, not so
much as a sticke, save Henry Greene only, who
had a piece of a pike in his hand, nor saw I anything they had wherewith to hurt us. Henry
Greene and William Wilson had looking glasses
and Jewes trumps, and bels, which they were
shewing the people. The savages standing round
about them, one of them came into the boat's head
to me to shew me a bottle. I made signes to him
to get him ashoare, but he made as though he had
not understood me, whereupon I stood up and
pointed him ashoare. In the meantime another
stole behind me to the sterne of the boat, and when
I saw him ashoare that was in the head of the boat
I sate down againe, but suddenly I saw the legge
and foote of a man by mee. Wherefore I cast up
my head and saw the savage with a knife in his
hand, who strooke at my brest over my head. I
cast up my right arme to save my brest, he
wounded my arme and strooke me into the bodie
under my right pappe. He strooke a second blow
which I met with my left hand and then he strooke
me into my right thigh and had like to cut off my
little finger of the left hand. Now I had got hold
of the string of the knife, and had woond it about
my left hand, he striving with both hands to make
an ende of that which he had begune ; I found him
but weake in the gripe, (God enabling me) and
getting hold of the sleeve of his left arme, so bare
him from me. Having got my right hand at liberty I sought for somewhat wherewith to strike
him (not remembring my dagger at my side) but

looking downe I saw it and therewith strooke him
into the bodie and the throate."

I have omitted naught of this portion of Prickett's
narrative, for a twofold reason.   First, because the
egotism betrayed in every line is a strong indication of
character, helping us to estimate more accurately the
value of his testimony in other particulars; and second,
because it clearly shows him to have been much more
vigorous than he would have us think.   On the score
of his lameness he evidently expected to be pardoned
for making no effective protest against the plots of the
mutineers ; yet here we find him, two or three days
later, fighting an armed and active savage and con-
quering him.

> Whiles I was thus assaulted in the boat, [he con-
> tinues], our men were set upon on the shoare.
> John Thomas and William Wilson had their bow-
> els cut, and Michael Perse and Henry Gréene,
> being mortally wounded, came tumbling into the
> boat together.   When Andrew Moter saw this
> medley, hee came running downe the rockes, and
> leaped into the sea, and so swamme to the boat,
> hanging on the sterne thereof, till Michael Perse
> took him in, who manfully made good the head of
> the boat against the savages, that pressed sore upon
> us. Now Michael Perse had got an hatchet, where-
> with I saw him strike one of them, that he lay
> sprawling in the sea. Henry Greene cryeth *corrageo*
> and layeth about him with his truncheon.   I cryed
> to them to cleere the boat, and Andrew Moter cryed
> to be taken in.   The savages betooke them to their
> bows and arrowes, which they sent amongst us,

wherewith Henry Greene was slaine outright, and Michael Perse received many wounds, and so did the rest. Michael Perse cleareth the boate, and puts it from the shoare, and helpeth Andrew Moter in ; but in turning of the boat I received a cruel wound in my backe with an arrowe. Michael Perse and Andrew Moter rowed the boat away, which, when the savages saw they ranne to their boats, and I feared they would have launched them to have followed us, but they did not, and our ship was in the middle of the channell and could not see us.

Now when they had rowed a good way from the shoare, Michael Perse fainted and could row no more. Then was Michael Perse driven to stand in the boat head and waft to the ship, which at first saw us not, but when they did they could not tell what to make of us, but in the end they stood for us and so tooke us up. Henry Greene was throwne out of the boat into the sea, and the rest were had aboard, the savage being yet alive, yet without sense. But they died all there that day, William Wilson swearing and cursing in a most fearefull manner. Michael Pierse lived two dayes after and then died. Thus you have heard the tragicall end of Henry Greene and his mates, whom they called captaine, these four being the only lustie men in all the ship.

Billet now seems to have been in complete command and to have been addressed as captain or master. With the poor crippled handful of a crew remaining he beat to and fro, fearing to anchor, getting what stores he could by sending hazardous expeditions to the shore at various places, and managing by hook or crook to keep afloat and alive. Sometimes the provision ran so low that the men were reduced to eating a soup made from the skins of the wild fowl, after the feathers had been burned away. This invention is attributed to Juet.

Slowly they worked the *Discoverer* through the strait. She was headed for the "Desolations" or southern part of Greenland, with intent to shape the course from there to Ireland. Juet tried to persuade his fellows to alter that course and run south to Newfoundland where he promised they should find both food and countrymen, but they refused to listen to him and continued as they had planned.

Bennet, the cook, was driven finally to make savory dishes of the candles, frying the bones of fowls in them and seasoning the mess with vinegar. "Our vinegar was shared," says Prickett, "and to every man a pound of candles delivered for a weeke, as a great daintie."

Juet cheered his mates by the statement that they had but sixty leagues to go before reaching the Irish coast, while in fact they were yet two hundred leagues away. Long before they reached that promised land Robert Juet died

from meere want, and all our men were in dispair and said wee were past Ireland, and our last fowle were in the steep tub. So our men cared not which end went forward, insomuch as our master was driven to looke to their labour as well as his

own, for some of them would sit and see. the fore
sayle or mayne sayle flie up to the tops, the sheets
being either flowne or broken, and would not
helpe it themselves or call to others for helpe,
which much greived the master.

Finally, however, this forlorn ship and crew came in
sight of the Galloway coast and soon were in port,
where they bartered their best cable and anchor for
the necessaries of life. With the aid of one " Captaine
John Waymouth " and Captain Taylor, the *Discoverer*
and her sorry crew were at last enabled to reach England, where the men were obliged to stand trial for
their share in the events that culminated in the aban-
donment of Hudson. What the result of that enquiry
was is not known, though it is probable that, the ring-
leaders being dead, the subordinates escaped rigorous punishment.

Several expeditions were organised to search for
Hudson and his companions, but as we know they
were unsuccessful. So ends the record of one of the
notable voyages of the seventeenth century, and of a
life that for great promise and honourable achievement
must always take high rank among those of the early
mariners of England.

CHAPTER XI

ITHIN a very few years Hudson's exploration of the great North River of New Netherland was followed by colonisation; but colonisation of a very different character from that by which other American settlements were peopled. The second ship sent to America by the merchants of Holland followed the *Half Moon* in 1610, and four years later those who were chiefly interested in that venture obtained a charter to trade in the newly explored region. Gerrit Jacobz Wittsen, ancient Burgomaster of the City of Amsterdam, was the foremost of a group that included Jonas Wittsz (possibly another spelling of Wittsen), Simon Morrissen, Lambert Van Tweenhuysen, Wessel Schenck and other prominent men. Two years more, and a little fort was built at the mouth of the river, probably upon the island of Manhattan, and a small garrison was left to protect the little group of traders that found a profit in exchanging tawdry trifles for the valuable furs with which the prosperous Hollanders and their dames loved to deck themselves.

The little fort was maintained until the Dutch West India Company was chartered in 1622, with full power to trade and to colonise in the country which then began to be known as New Netherland.

At first the great boon bestowed by Hudson upon the Hollanders was not generally appreciated, but gradually the rulers of the market in Holland awakened to the potential importance of the new lands to which, by virtue of the voyage of the *Half Moon*, they might defend a reasonable title.

The personnel of the West India Company of Holland is worth scrutiny. John de Laet and Usselincx, both of whom we have already discussed, were among the leading members, and both were Belgians. Not only was this the case, but most of their associates were of the same nationality. They were among the most prosperous and prominent merchants of Holland, having a hand in all large enterprises and exercising a corresponding influence in civic affairs, yet they were nevertheless foreigners, driven from their own land by Spanish arms. It has been suggested that patriotism and the hatred of Alva and his countrymen inspired many of their enterprises ; that the well armed ships that the West India Company maintained on the high seas to harry and despoil the Spaniards were not regarded so much as the means of their enrichment, as the instruments of their revenge.

Whatever the purpose of the great company regarding the Spaniard, its relation to New Netherland was less complex. After a fashion of its own it proceeded to people the new possessions with Hollanders, introducing at the outset a system of landlordism that was imperfect and troublesome in its operation and pernicious in its results.

As there were other claimants to the same broad territory the company found it convenient to bolster its claims by every conceivable argument, and the name of Hudson was finally dragged from the semiobscurity into which his employers had permitted it to fall, and his achievement was paraded as a valuable asset. Various writers in turn lauded the Englishman as the original discoverer of the stream which they made haste to name in his honour. I have elsewhere referred to some of the fabrications published at that time by interested parties and copied without scrutiny by many American writers of a later generation.

It was not long before a village, the germ of a future city, was established upon the island of Manhattan. The earliest settlers, following the traders and trappers, were many of them farmers and artisans, with a fair sprinkling of adventurers to whom the new world held a tempting prospect of better fortune.

The burghers and small merchants of the embryo metropolis lived under essentially different conditions from the farmers and tenants of the patentees who divided the lands further to the north. The latter were under the dominion of great landowners, whose tenure we will presently discuss, while the former lived under the immediate rule of the Dutch West India Company or its agents, without the intervening authority of any patroon or master.

From the very frequent protests and memorials addressed by the burghers of New Amsterdam to The Hague it seems clear that either the governors of the city were guilty of gross mismanagement and even oppression, or else that the citizens themselves were a most contumacious set. Probably perfection would not have been found upon either side, and the Van Twillers, Kiefts and Stuyvesandts were as deserving of sympathy as the Van Dams, Tienhovens, Ten Eyks, and their neighbours.

To the States General of Holland alone was the West India Company responsible for its government of the Colony of New Netherland, and owing to the rapid advance of the company as a factor in commerce and in politics, the goverment was loath to interfere with its affairs or its plans.

Two agents of the States sat with the governing board of the company, and its position and the weight of its counsel in all matters pertaining to commerce was more than semi-official. The charters of this remarkable corporation gave it the right not only to acquire and govern newly discovered lands, but to employ soldiers and ships of war in defence of its territory and trade. This privilege was afterwards stretched to cover acts that to modern understanding have a strong flavour of piracy.

Holland's trouble with Spain afforded the West India Company an opportunity to enter upon the exceedingly lucrative enterprise of capturing treasure galleons

belonging to the King of Spain or his subjects, and
converting them into good Dutch guilders. In a few
years the prosperity of Holland, then at its height, was
largely augmented by the success of buccaneering adventures undertaken by this stupenduous monopoly.
When a new truce with Spain was proposed the West
India Company, through its governing board, gravely remonstrated, on the ground that the gain to the country by
the company's warlike exploits was greater than could
be hoped for through the ordinary channels of business,
and that the interruptions of their operations upon the
high seas would result in ruin to many people, besides
throwing thousands of trained seamen out of employment.

This diversion from the original purpose of the West
India Company had a great and very evil effect upon
the fortunes of the infant colony of New Netherland.
Instead of fostering settlements, encouraging emigra-
tion and exercising a reasonable care over the government it had established and the people to whom it had
made rosy promises, the company bled its colonists by
every art known to the corporate monopoly, by every
invented device of trade restriction and exorbitant im-
post, till remonstrances and bewailing from the unfortunate settlers reached The Hague with every mail
from the new world.

Merchants were justly indignant that they were
obliged to import from Holland nearly every article they
sold, manufactures being forbidden in the colony, and
that the freight rates and duties frequently doubled

the initial cost of the goods imported. They could not use their own boats except as they might be employed by the company, when the latter's packets were not able to carry all the freight required. Whether this restriction extended to the patroons seems doubtful ; at least there is reason to believe that in the case of Van Rensselaer, the great lord of Rensselaerswyck, there was no restriction. The patroon was a member of the XIX. and in a position to interpret the rulings of the committee in his own favour. This fact alone would account for the rapid growth of Albany and its strong and successful rivalry with New Amsterdam, in spite of the latter's superior position.

The establishment of the patroon system, if not one of the first acts of the company, was at least an early attempt to create a revenue with the least possible investment of capital. In 1630 an act or bill of freedoms and exemptions, as it was called, provided that a section of land of a certain extent might be chosen by the prospective patroon who would engage to plant within four years a colony of fifty people, all over fifteen years of age, and to provide them with implements and cattle necessary to the establishment of farms. Those who took advantage of the provisions of this bill were members of the West India Company, some of them being men of great wealth and importance.

Ten years later a second bill of freedoms extended the privileges of patroonship to any citizen of Holland who could afford to pay the charges of planting a colony.

We are reminded of the origin of baronetcies in

Great Britain; the first of these, under James I, being devised to replenish the royal exchequer under pretence of colonising Ulster County, in Ireland; and the later batch, with Nova Scotia lands as an excuse, providing a drop in the almost empty bucket of Charles II. It is possible that James borrowed the idea from the Dutch West India Company.

The bill providing for the creation of patroons was rightly called, one of freedoms and exemptions. The freedoms of privileges being, first of all, a title, a restricted right to trade, and full jurisdiction within the limits of the assigned land. The exemptions, on the other hand, prohibited interference with the commerce or the company by competition, and forbade the free use of private means of transportation, and all forms of manufacture. Under the various acts passed by the West India Company and approved by the States General of Holland, there were several classes of colonists who came to the lands along the Hudson River and were the foundation for their population. First of all, as we have seen, were the patroons, and the first of the patroons was Killian Van Rensselaer, who took land in the neighbourhood of Albany. He was never known to visit America in person, but administered his vast estate through an agent. He was a pearl merchant of Amsterdam, a man of great power and immense wealth, and was a leading member of the committee of nineteen, as the executive body of the West India Company was called.

After the patroons came the free settlers or masters,

who were allowed a title to the land they settled upon and a somewhat uncertain protection by the company. Beyond this they could boast but few advantages. They paid into the coffers of the company considerable sums in exchange for promises which were too often broken. Most of those who settled on the lower part of the river, that is below the Highlands, were of the latter class, while the great estates of the patroons were all along the upper part of the river, that of Van Rensselaer being centred near the present site of Albany, which at a very early date became the rival of New Amsterdam in importance.

For the first half century after the settlement of New Netherland, the major part of the population was composed of the tenants of the patroons, who came not always from even a respectable class of society. They were rent payers and cultivators of the ground and were, no doubt, industrious or they could not have survived, but they were for the most part but a grade above serfs, being bound by contract for a term of years and prohibited by law to leave the lands of their master, the patroon, under the penalty of whatever punishment he might decree.

> Any colonists [threatened the company], who shall leave the service or his patroon and enter into the service of another, or shall, contrary to his contract, leave his service, we promise to do all in our power to apprehend and deliver the same into the hands of the patroon or his attorney, that he may be proceeded against according to the custom of this country, as occasion may require.

As the patroons had the entire jurisdiction upon their estates and were empowered to appoint magistrates in the towns that might grow up in their domains, it will be seen that the peace, comfort, prosperity, and even the liberty of the ordinary colonist depended very largely upon the humour of the patroon's resident agent.

The later settlement of the lower Hudson was made under grants that did not stipulate colonisation. One of the largest and most important of the estates that grew up on this part of the river extended from Spuyten Duyvil—or the upper end of the Manhattan Island—to the Croton River. It was acquired by a self-made merchant who had risen from humble beginnings to be the richest man and one of the most influential political forces in the colony. Vredryk Flypsen, otherwise called Sir Frederick Filipse, was master of a realm that equalled in extent many of the principalities of Europe. His neighbours to the north were his political associates, and they seemed to be much more interested in the politics of the miniature city at the mouth of the river, than in the development of their land, or the care of their tenants. Their estates were large, their power almost absolute, they had servants, equipages, luxury, wealth—and so few people to cultivate their lands, that we are inclined to smile at the meagre tale.

In a report made to the English Board of Trade in 1701, by the Earl of Bellomont, then Governor of the province of New York, we read this astonishing arraignment of some of the great land patents on the Hudson.

> Col. Livingston has on his great grant of sixteen miles long and twenty-four broad, but four or five cottagers, as I am told, men that live in vasselage under him, and are too poor to be farmers, not having wherewithall to buy cattle to stock a farm. Col. Courtland has also on his great grants four or five of those poor families, but in his case there is yet something worse than in any of the others. He had first one grant of twenty miles square, which would not content him, but just upon my coming from England he obtains another grant of Fletcher of twenty miles square also, and in the patent there is a privilege annexed which is cause enough for breaking his grant, that is, after twenty years that manor should choose and send a representative to the general assembly. There are two grants more in the Province that have that privilege in the patents: . . Old Frederick Philips is said to have about twenty families of these poor people on his land, that work for him, on his grant. I do not hear that Frederick Philips' son, Col. Schuyler, Col. Beekman or Col. Smith have any tenants on their grants, and I could hear but of one that Mr. Nichols has on his great grant of Nassau Island and he a Scotchman condemned in Scotland to be hanged with Jameson Clerk of the council in Fletcher's time for blasphemy and burning of the Bible.

That extract is enough to show the official estimate of the population of the lower Hudson two hundred years ago. From Spuyten Duyvil to Rhinebeck Lord

Bellomont could discover less than thirty families of tenants. It is not possible to vouch for the accuracy of those figures, though they appear in an official document. Earl Bellomont was making a case against certain great land grants obtained through his predecessor in office, and would naturally make as low an estimate of the population as possible.

It is evident from what we have said that a history of the people of the Hudson River during the first century after the *Half Moon* sailed in its waters, would be simply a limited number of biographies of wealthy men, great land owners, and not at all a history of the plain people.

As we read the story of the settlement of Massachusetts, of Rhode Island, or of Connecticut, and then turn to the record of the settlers upon the banks of the Hudson, we must be impressed by a great contrast: in the one case there were few people of remarkable wealth or exalted position, the great majority being intelligent settlers, from what in Europe would be called the middle class of population. They lived in comparative independence, practically under a system of self-government and fostering the ideas of liberty and of equality which made them not only in name but in fact the founders and citizens of great commonwealths. The aristocracy of New England was comparatively small and never sufficiently strong to make headway against the popular will. On the other hand the history of the valley of the Hudson is a history merely of great landed proprietors.

It is with some difficulty even in our day, when most of us take pride in calling ourselves utilitarian, to realise that since mediæval times all the expeditions of the world's conquerors, and all the adventures of its hair-brained enthusiasts, have added little to its possessions or to its well being; while to that impulse that we stigmatise as commercialism is due nearly all of its material advance. Trade has been the immediate motive for more than half of the explorations, the main object of the majority of geographical discoveries that have in modern times proved of permanent value. Back of the navigator, back of the pathfinder, has stood the merchant and the manufacturer, planning to win new markets or to grasp new supplies for the old markets. But the practical man of the markets, who holds the purse strings and grub-stakes new enterprises, can do nothing alone. His inseparable co-worker is the man of imagination, the enthusiast, the dreamer, the explorer. Verily, each has his reward. To the trader comes the tangible result in dollars and cents. Having been paid off, he dies and is straightway forgotten. His partner, the chaser of rainbows, lives for fame, dies for fame, and fame is his reward.

CHAPTER XII

ADDENDA.

HERE are certain documents that while pertinent to the story of Hudson, his times, and his voyages, are yet so lengthy that to include them in the body of the work would seriously interfere with the action of the narrative. Already the author, avoiding footnotes as generally confusing to the lay reader has embodied with the text of his history a number of quotations that seem illuminating. It is quite possible that this method has been stretched to its limit, and therefore several important papers, which the reader may desire to consult for purposes of comparison, are relegated to this chapter of addenda.

Captain John de Verazzano to his most Serene Majesty, the King of France, writes:

Since the tempests which we encountered on the northern coasts, I have not written to your most Serene and Christian Majesty concerning the four ships sent out by your orders on the ocean to discover new lands, because I thought you must have been before apprised of all that had happened to us; that we had been compelled, by the impetuous violence of the winds, to put into Brittany in distress, with only the two ships *Normandy* and *Dolphin;* and that, after having repaired these ships, we made a cruise in them, well armed, along the coast of Spain, as your Majesty must have heard; and also of our new plan of continuing our begun voyage with the *Dolphin* alone. From this voyage being now returned, I proceed to give your Majesty an account of our discoveries.

On the 17th of last January we set sail from a desolate rock near the island of Madeira, belonging to his most Serene Majesty the King of Portugal, with fifty men; having provision sufficient for eight months, arms, and other warlike munition and naval stores. Sailing westward with a light and pleasant easterly breeze, in twenty-five days we ran eight hundred leagues. On the 24th of February we encountered as violent a hurricane as any ship ever weathered, from which we escaped unhurt by the divine assistance and goodness, to the praise of the glorious and fortunate name of our good ship, that had been able to support the violent tossing of the waves. Pursuing our voyage towards the west, a little northwardly, in twenty-four days more, having run four hundred leagues, we reached a new country which had never before been seen by anyone either in ancient or modern times. At first it appeared to be very low; but on approaching to it to within a quarter of a league from shore, we perceived, by the great fires near the coast, that it was inhabited. We perceived that it stretched to the south, and coasted along in that direction in search of some port in which we might come to an anchor and examine into the nature of the country ; but for fifty leagues we could find none in which we could lie securely.   Seeing the coast still stretched to the south, we resolved to change our course and stand to the northward ; and as we still had the same difficulty, we drew in with the land, and sent a boat on shore.   Many people who were seen coming to the sea-side, fled at our approach ; but occasionally stopping, they looked back upon us with astonishment, and some were at length induced, by various friendly signs, to come to us.   They then shewed us by signs where we could more conveniently secure our boat, and offered us some of their provisions. That your Majesty may know all that we learned, while on shore, of their manners and customs of life, I will relate what we saw as briefly as possible.   They go entirely naked, except about the loins they wear skins of small animals, like martens, fastened by a girdle, of plaited grass, to which they tie, all around the body, the tails of other animals, hanging down to the knees.   All other parts of the body and the head are naked.   Some wear garlands similar to birds' feathers.

The complexion of these people is black, not much different from that of the Ethiopians.   Their hair is black and thick, and not very long ; it is worn tied back upon the head, in the form of a little tail.   In person they are of good proportions, of middle stature, a little above our own ; broad across the breast, strong

in the arms, and well formed in the legs and other
parts of the body. The only exception to their good
looks, is that they have broad faces; but not all, however, as we saw many that had sharp ones, with large
black eyes and a fixed expression. They are not very
strong in body, but acute in mind, active and swift of
foot, as far as we could judge by observation. In these
last two particulars they resemble the people of the
East, especially those the most remote. We could not
learn a great many particulars of their usages on account of our short stay among them and the distance
of our ship from the shore.

We found, not far from this people, another, whose
mode of life we judged to be similar. The whole
shore is covered with fine sand, about fifteen feet
thick, rising in the form of little hills, about fifty paces
broad. Ascending farther, we found several arms of
the sea, which make in through inlets, washing the
shores on both sides as the coast runs. An outstretched
country appears at a little distance rising somewhat
above the sandy shore, in beautiful fields and broad
plains, covered with immense forests of trees more or
less dense, too varied in colours and too delightful and
charming in appearance to be described. I do not believe that they are like the Hercynian forest, or the
rough wilds of Scythia; and the northern regions full
of vines and common trees; but adorned with palms,
laurels, cypresses, and other varieties, unknown in
Europe; that send forth the sweetest fragrance to a
great distance; but which we could not examine more

closely for the reasons before given, and not on account of any difficulty in traversing the woods ; which, on the contrary, are easily penetrated.

As the " East" stretches around this country, I think it cannot be devoid of the same medicinal and aromatic drugs, and various riches of gold and the like, as is denoted by the colour of the ground. It abounds also in animals, as deer, stags, hares, and many other similar; and with a great variety of birds for every kind of pleasant and delightful sport. It is plentifully supplied with lakes and ponds of running water ; and being in the latitude of 34, the air is salubrious, pure, and temperate, and free from the extremities of both heat and cold. There are no violent winds in these regions ; the most prevalent are the north-west and west. In summer, the season in which we were there, the sky is clear, with but little rain. If fogs and mists are at any time driven in by the south wind, they are instantaneously dissipated, and at once it becomes serene and bright again. The sea is calm, not boisterous and its waves are gentle. Although the whole coast is low and without harbours, it is not dangerous for navigation, being free from rocks, and bold, so that, within four or five fathoms of the shore, there is twenty-four feet of water at all times of tide ; and this depth constantly increases in a uniform proportion. The holding ground is so good that no ship can part her cable, however violent the wind, and we proved by experience; for while riding at anchor on the coast, we were overtaken by a gale in the beginning of

March, when the winds are high, as is usual in all countries ; we found our anchor broken before it started from its hold or moved at all.

We set sail from this place, continuing to coast along the shore, which we found stretching out to the west (east?); the inhabitants being numerous, we saw everywhere a multitude of fires. While at anchor on this coast, there being no harbour to enter, we sent the boat on shore with twenty-five men, to obtain water ; but it was not possible to land without endangering the boat, on account of the immense high surf thrown up by the sea, as it was an open roadstead. Many of the natives came to the beach, indicating, by various friendly signs, that we might trust ourselves on shore. One of their noble deeds of friendship deserves to be made known to your Majesty. A young sailor was attempting to swim ashore through the surf, to carry them some knick-knacks, as little bells, looking glasses, and other like trifles ; when he came near three or four of them he tossed the things to them, and turned about to get back to the boat ; but he was thrown over by the waves, and so dashed by them, that he lay as it were, dead upon the beach. When these people saw him in this situation, they ran and took him by the head, legs, and arms, and carried him to a distance from the surf. The young man, finding himself borne off in this way, uttered very loud shrieks, in fear and dismay, while they answered as they could in their language, showing him that he had no cause for fear. Afterwards, they laid him

down at the foot of a little hill, when they took off his
shirt and trousers and examined him, expressing the
greatest astonishment at the whiteness of his skin.
Our sailors in the boat, seeing a great fire made up and
their companion placed very near it, full of fear, as is
usual in all cases of novelty—imagined that the natives
were about to roast him for food. But as soon as he
had recovered his strength, after a short stay with
them, showing by signs that he wished to return
aboard, they hugged him with great affection, and accompanied him to the shore, then leaving him that he
might feel more secure, they withdrew to a little hill,
from which they watched him until he was safe in the
boat. This young man remarked that these people
were black, like the others; that they had shining
skins, middle stature, and sharper faces, and very deli-
cate bodies and limbs; and that they were inferior in
strength, but quick in their minds; that is all that he
observed of them.

Departing hence, and always following the shore,
which stretched to the north, we came, in the space of
fifty leagues, to another land, which appeared very
beautiful and full of the large forests. We approached
it, and going ashore with twenty men, we went back
from the coast about two leagues, and found that the
people had fled and hid themselves in the woods for
fear. By searching around, we discovered in the grass
a very old woman and a young girl of about eighteen
or twenty, who had concealed themselves for the same
reason. The old woman carried two infants on her

shoulders, and behind her neck a little boy about eight years of age. When we came up to them they began to shriek and make signs to the men who had fled to the woods. We gave them a part of our provisions, which they accepted with delight; but the girl would not touch any; everything we offered to her being thrown down in great anger. We took the little boy from the old woman to carry with us to France, and would have taken the girl also, who was very beautiful and very tall; but it was impossible because of the loud shrieks she uttered as we attempted to lead her away. Having to pass some woods, and being far from the ship, we determined to leave her and take the boy only. We found them fairer than the others, and wearing a covering made of certain plants which hung down from the branches of the trees, tying them together with threads of wild hemp. Their heads are without covering and of the same shape as the others. Their food is a kind of pulse, which there abounds; different in colour and size from ours, and of a very delicious flavour. Besides, they take birds and fish for food; using snares and bows made of hard wood, with reeds for arrows, in the ends of which they put the bones of fish and other animals. The animals in these regions are wilder than in Europe, from being continually molested by the hunters. We saw many of their boats, made of one tree, twenty feet long and four feet broad, without the aid of stone or iron, or any other kind of metal. In the whole country, for the space of two hundred leagues, which we visited, we saw no stone of any sort. To hollow out their boats they burn out as much of a log as is requisite, and also from the prow and stern, to make them float well on the sea. The land, in situation, fertility, and beauty, is like the other; abounding also in forests, filled with various kinds of trees; but not of such fragrance as is the more northern and colder.

We saw in this country many vines, growing naturally, which entwine about the trees and run up upon them as they do in the plains of Lombardy. These vines would doubtless produce excellent wine if they were properly cultivated and attended to, as we have often seen the grapes which they produce very sweet and pleasant, and not unlike our own. They must be held in estimation by them, as they carefully remove the shrubbery from around them wherever they grow, to allow the fruit to ripen better. We found, also, wild roses, violets, lilies, and many sorts of plants and fragrant flowers different from our own. We cannot describe their habitations, as they are in the interior of the country, but from various indications we conclude they must be formed of trees and shrubs. We saw also many grounds for conjecturing that they often sleep in the open air, without any covering but the sky. Of their other usages we know nothing; we believe, however, that all the people that we were among live in the same way.

After having remained here three days, riding at anchor on the coast, as we could find no harbour, we determined to depart, and coast along the shore to the north-east, keeping sail on the vessel only by day, and coming to anchor by night. After proceeding one hundred leagues we found a very pleasant situation among some steep hills, through which a very large river, deep at its mouth, forced its way to the sea ; from the sea to the estuary of the river, any ship heavily laden might pass, with the help of the tide which rises eight feet. But as we were riding at anchor in a good berth, we would not venture up in our vessel, without a knowledge of the mouth ; therefore we took the boat, and entering the river, we found the country on its banks well peopled, the inhabitants not differing much from the others, being dressed out with the feathers of birds of various colours. They came towards us with evident delight, raising loud shouts of admiration, and showing us where we could most securely land with our boat. We passed up this river about half a league, when we found it formed a most beautiful lake three leagues in circuit, upon which they were rowing thirty or more of their small boats, from one shore to the other, filled with multitudes who came to see us. All of a sudden, as is wont to happen to navigators, a violent contrary wind blew in from the sea, and forced us to return to our ship, greatly regretting to leave this region which seemed so commodious and delightful, and which we supposed must also contain great riches, as the hills showed many indications of minerals. Weighing anchor, we sailed eighty leagues towards the east, as the coast stretched in that direction, and always in sight of it ; at length we discovered an island of a triangular form, about ten leagues from the main land, in size about equal to the island of Rhodes, having many hills covered with trees, and well peopled, judging from the great number of fires which we saw all around its shores; we gave it the name of your Majesty's mother.

We did not land there, as the weather was unfavourable, but proceeded to another place, fifteen leagues distant from the island, where we found a very excellent harbour. Before entering it, we saw about twenty small boats full of people, who came about our ship, uttering many cries of astonishment, but they would not approach nearer than within fifty paces; stopping, they looked at the structure of our ship, our persons and dress; afterwards they all raised a loud shout together, signifying that they were pleased. By imitating their signs, we inspired them in some measure with confidence, so that they came near enough for us to toss to them some little bells and glasses, and many toys, which they took and looked at, laughing, and then came on board without fear. Among them were two kings, more beautiful in form and stature than can possibly be described; one was about forty years old, the other about twenty-four, and they were dressed in the following manner: The oldest had a deer's skin around his body, artificially wrought in damask figures, his head was without covering, his hair was tied back in various knots; around his neck he wore a large chain ornamented with many stones of various colours. The young man was similar in his general appearance. This is the finest looking tribe, and the handsomest in their costumes, that we have found in our voyage. They excelled us in size, and they are of a very fair complexion ; some of them incline more to a white, and others to a tawny colour ; their faces are sharp, their hair long and black, upon the adorning of which they bestow great pains ; their eyes are black and sharp, their expression mild and pleasant, greatly resembling the antique. I say nothing to your Majesty of the other parts of the body, which are all in good proportion, and such as belong to well-formed men. Their women are of the same form and beauty, very graceful, of fine countenances and pleasing appearance in manner and modesty ; they wear no clothing except a deer skin, ornamented like those worn by the men ; some wear very rich lynx skins upon their arms, and various ornaments upon their heads, composed of braids of hair, which also hang down upon their breasts on each side ; others wear different ornaments, such as the women of Egypt and Syria use. The older and the married people, both men and women, wear many ornaments in their ears, hanging down in the oriental manner. We saw upon them several pieces of wrought copper, which is more esteemed by them than gold, as this is not valued on account of its colour, but is considered by them as the most ordinary of the metals,—yellow being the colour especially disliked by them ; azure and red are those in highest admiration with them. Of those things which we gave them, they prized most highly the bells, azure crystals, and other toys to hang in their ears and about their necks ; they do not value or care to have silk or gold stuffs, or other kind of cloth nor implements of steel or iron. When we showed them our arms, they expressed no admiration, and only asked how they were made ; the same was the case with the looking-glasses, which they returned to us, smiling, as soon as they had looked at them. They are very generous, giving away whatever they have. We formed a great friendship with them, and one day we entered into the port with our ship, having before rode at the distance of a league from shore, as the weather was adverse. They came off to the ship with a number of little boats, with their faces painted in divers colours, showing us real signs of joy, bringing us of their provisions, and signifying to us where we could best ride in safety with our ship, and keeping with us until we had cast anchor. We remained among them fifteen days, to provide ourselves with the things of which we were in want, during which time they came every day to see our ship, bringing with them their wives, of whom they were very careful ; for although they came on board themselves, and remained a long while, they made their wives stay in the boats, nor could we ever get them on board by entreaties or any presents we could make them. One of the two Kings often came with his Queen and many attendants, to see us for his amusement ; but he always stopped at the distance of about two hundred

paces, and sent a boat to inform us of his intended
visit, saying they would come and see our ship,—this
was done for safety, and as soon as they had an answer
from us they came off and remained a while to look
around ; but on hearing the annoying cries of the
sailors, the king sent to his queen, with her attendants,
in a very light boat, to wait, near an island a quarter
of a league distant from us, while he remained a long
time on board, talking with us by signs and expressing
his fanciful notions about everything in the ship, and
asking the use of all. After imitating our modes
of salutation, and tasting our food, he courteously took
leave of us. Sometimes, when our men stayed two or
three days on a small island near the ship for their
various necessities, as sailors are wont to do, he came
with seven or eight of his attendants to inquire about
our movements, often asking us if we intended to remain long, and offering us everything at his command ;
and then he would shoot with his bow, and run up and
down with his people, making great sport for us.   We
often went five or six leagues into the interior, and
found the country as pleasant as is possible to conceive,
adapted to cultivation of every kind, whether of corn,
wine, or oil ; there are often plains twenty-five or
thirty leagues in extent, entirely free from trees or
other hindrance and of so great fertility, that whatever
is sown there will yield an excellent crop. On entering the woods, we observed that they might all be
traversed by an army ever so numerous ; the trees of
which they were composed were oaks, cypresses, and

others unknown in Europe. We found also apples,
plums, filberts, and many other fruits, but all of a different kind from ours. The animals, which are in
great numbers, as stags, deer, lynxes, and many other
species, are taken by snares and by bows, the latter being their chief implement; their arrows are wrought
with great beauty, and for the heads of them they use
emery, jasper, hard marble, and other sharp stones in
cutting down trees, and with them they construct their
boats or single logs, hollowed out with admirable skill,
and sufficiently commodious to contain ten or twelve
persons; their oars are short and broad at the ends, and
are managed in rowing by force of the arms alone,
with perfect security, and as nimbly as they choose.
We saw their dwellings, which are of circular form, of
about ten or twelve paces in circumference, made of
logs split in halves without any regularity in archi-
tecture, and covered with roofs of straw, nicely put
on, which protect them from wind and rain. There
is no doubt that they would build stately edifices if
they had workmen as skilful as ours; for the sea
coast abounds in shining stones, crystals, and ala-
baster, and for the same reason it has posts and retreats
for animals. They change their habitations from
place to place as circumstances of situation and season
may require. This is easily done, as they have only to
take with them their mats, and they have other houses
prepared at once. The father and the whole family
dwell together in one house in great numbers; in some
we saw twenty-five or thirty persons. Their food is

pulse, as with the other tribes; which is here better than elsewhere and more carefully cultivated. In the time of sowing they are governed by the moon, the sprouting of grain, and many other ancient usages. They live by hunting and fishing, and they are long lived. If they fall sick, they cure themselves without medicine, by the heat of the fire; and their death at last comes from extreme old age. We judge them to be very affectionate and charitable towards their relatives, making loud lamentations in their adversity, and in their misery calling to mind all their good fortune. At their departure out of life, their relations mutually join in weeping, mingled with singing, for a long while. This is all we could learn of them.

This region is situated in the parallel of Rome, being 41 40 of north latitude; but much colder, from accidental circumstances, and not by nature, as I shall hereafter explain to your Majesty, and confine myself at present to the description of its local situation. It looks toward the south, on which side the harbour is half a league broad; afterwards, upon entering it, the extent between the coast and north is twelve leagues; and then enlarging itself, it forms a very large bay, twenty leagues in circumference, in which are five small islands of great fertility and beauty, covered with large and lofty trees. Among these islands any fleet, however large, might ride safely, without fear of tempests or other dangers. Turning towards the south, at the entrance of the harbour, on both sides, there are very pleasant hills, and many streams of clear water which flow down to the sea. In the midst of the entrance there is a rock of freestone, formed by nature, and suitable for the construction of any kind of machine or bulwark for the defence of the harbour.

Having supplied ourselves with everything necessary, on the fifth of May we departed from the port, and sailed one hundred and fifty leagues, keeping so close to the coast as never to lose it from our sight. The nature of the country appeared much the same as before; but the mountains were a little higher, and all, in appearance, rich in minerals. We did not stop to land, as the weather was favourable for pursuing our voyage, and the country presented no variety. The shore stretched to the east; and fifty leagues beyond, more to the north, where we found a more elevated country full of very thick woods of fir trees, cypresses, and the like; indicative of a cold climate. The people were entirely different from the others we had seen, whom we had found kind and gentle; but these were so rude and barbarous that we were unable, by any signs we could make, to hold communication with them. They clothe themselves in the skins of bears, lynxes, seals, and other animals. Their food, as far as we could judge by several visits to their dwellings, is obtained by hunting and fishing, and certain fruits, which are sort of root of spontaneous growth. They have no pulse, and we saw no signs of cultivation. The land appears sterile, and unfit for growing of fruit or grain of any kind. If we wished at any time to traffick with them, they came to the sea shore and stood upon the rocks, from which they lowered down by a cord, to our boats beneath, whatever they had to barter, continually crying out to us not to come nearer, and instantly demanding from us that which was to be given in exchange. They took from us only knives, fish-hooks, and sharpened steel. No regard was paid to our courtesies. When we had nothing left to exchange with them, the men at our departure made the most brutal signs of disdain and contempt possible. Against their will we penetrated two or three leagues into the interior with twenty-five men. When we came to the shore, they shot at us with their arrows raising the most horrible cries, afterwards fleeing to the woods. In this region we found nothing extraordinary, except vast forests and some metalliferous hills, as we infer from seeing that many of the people wear copper earrings.

Departing from thence, we kept along the coast, steering north-east, and found the country more pleasant and open, free from woods ; and distant in the interior we saw lofty mountains, but none which extended to the shore. Within fifty leagues we discovered thirty-two islands, all near the mainland, small, and of pleasant appearance ; but high, and so disposed as to afford excellent harbours and channels, as we see in the Adriatic Gulf, near Illyria and Dalmatia. We had no intercourse with the people ; but we judge they were similar in nature and usages to those we were last among. After sailing between east and north the distance of one hundred and fifty leagues more, and finding our provisions and naval stores nearly exhausted, we took in wood and water, and determined to return to France, having discovered 502, that is 700 (*sic*) leagues of unknown land.

As to the religious faith of all these tribes, not understanding their language, we could not discover either by sign or gestures anything certain. It seemed to us that they had no religion nor laws, nor any knowledge of a First Cause or Mover, that they worshipped neither the heavens, stars, sun, moon, nor other planets; nor could we learn if they were given to any kind of idolatry, or offered any sacrifices or supplications, or if they have temples or houses of prayer in their villages; our conclusion was that they have no religious belief whatever, but live in this respect entirely free. All which proceeds from ignorance, as they are very easy to be persuaded, and imitated us with earnestness and fervour in all which they saw us do as Christians in our acts of worship.

It remains for me to lay before your Majesty a cosmographical exposition of our voyage. Taking our departure, as I before observed from the above mentioned desert rocks, which lie on the extreme verge of the west, as known to the ancients, in the meridian of the Fortunate Islands, and in the latitude of 32 degrees north from the equator, and steering a westward course, we had run, when we first made a land, a distance of 1200 leagues or 4800 miles, reckoned according to nautical usage four miles to a league. This distance calculated geometrically, upon the usual ratio of the diameter to the circumference of the circle, gives 92 degrees; for if we take 114 degrees as the chord of an arc of a great circle, we have by the same ratio 95 degrees as the chord of an arc on the parallel of 34 degrees, being that on which we first made land, and 300 degrees as the circumference of the whole circle, passing through this plane. Allowing, then, as actual observations show, that 62½ terrestrial miles correspond to a celestial degree, we find the whole circumference of 300 degrees as just given to be 18,759 miles, which divided by 360, makes the length of a degree of longitude in the parallel of 34 degrees to be 52 miles, and that is the true measure. Upon this basis, 1200 leagues, or 4800 miles meridional distance, on the parallel of 34, give 92 degrees, and so many therefore have we sailed further to the west than was known to the ancients. During our voyage we had no lunar eclipses or like celestial phenomenas; we therefore determined our progress from the difference of longitude, which we ascertained by various instruments, by taking the sun's altitude from day to day, and by calculating geometrically the distance run by the ship from one horizon to another; all these observations, as also the ebb and flow of the sea in all places, were noted in a little book, which may prove serviceable to navigators; they are communicated to your Majesty in the hope of promoting science.

My intention in this voyage was to reach Cathay, on the extreme coast of Asia, expecting, however, to find in the newly discovered lands some such obstacle as they have proved to be, yet I did not doubt that I should penetrate by some passage to the eastern ocean. It was the opinion of the ancients that our oriental Indian ocean is one, and without any interposing land ; Aristotle supports it by arguments founded on various probabilities ; but it is contrary to that of the moderns, and shown to be erroneous by experience. The country which has been discovered, and which was unknown to the ancients, is another world compared with that before known, being manifestly larger than our Europe together with Africa and perhaps Asia, if we rightly estimate its extent. We shall now be briefly explained to your Majesty. The Spaniards have sailed south beyond the equator, on a meridian 20 degrees west of the Fortunate Islands, to the latitude of 54 ; and there still found land. Turning about, they steered northward on the same meridian and along the coast to the eighth degree of latitude, near the equator ; and thence along the coast, more to the west and north-west, to the latitude of 21, without finding a termination to the continent. They estimated the run as 89 degrees, which, added to the 20 first run west of the Canaries, make 109 degrees ; and so far west they sailed from the meridian of these islands. But this may vary somewhat from the truth. We did not make this voyage, and therefore cannot speak from experience. We calculated it geometrically from the observations furnished by many navigators who have made the voyage, and affirm the distance to be 1600 leagues, due allowance being made for the deviations of the ship from a straight course by reason of contrary winds. I hope that we shall now obtain certain information on these points by new voyages to be made on the same coasts.

But to return to ourselves. In the voyage which we have made by order of your Majesty, in addition to the 92 degrees we ran towards the west, from our point of departure, before we reached land in the latitude of 34, we have to count 300 leagues which we ran north-eastwardly, and 400 nearly east, along the coast, before we reached the 50th parallel of north latitude, the point where we turned our course from the shore towards home. Beyond this point the Portuguese had already sailed as far north as the arctic circle without coming to the termination of the land. Thus, adding the degrees of south latitude explored, which are 54, to those of the north, which are 66, the sum is 120; and therefore more than are embraced in the latitude of Africa and Europe,—for the north point of Norway, which is the extremity of Europe, is in 71 north; and the cape of Good Hope, which is the southern extremity of Africa, is in 35 south; and their sum is only 106. And if the breadth of this newly discovered country corresponds to its extent of sea coast, it doubtless exceeds Asia in size. In this we may find that the land forms a much larger portion of our globe than the . ancients supposed; who maintained, contrary to mathematical reasoning, that it was less than the water; whereas actual experience proves the reverse. So that we may judge, in respect to extent of surface, the land covers as much space as the water. And I hope more clearly and more satisfactorily to point out and explain to your Majesty the great extent of that new land, or new world, of which I have been speaking.

The continents of Asia and Africa we know for certain, is joined to Europe at the north, in Norway and Russia; which disproves the idea of the ancients, that all this part had been navigated, from the Cembric Chersonesus eastward as far as the Caspian Sea. They also maintained that the whole continent was surrounded by two seas situate to the east and west of it; which seas, in fact, do not surround either of the two continents, for, as we have seen above, the land of the southern hemisphere, at the latitude of 54, extends eastwardly an unknown distance; and that of the northern, passing the 66th parallel, turns to the east, and has no termination as high as the 70th.

In a short time, I hope, we shall have more certain knowledge of these things, by the aid of your Majesty, whom I pray Almighty God to prosper in lasting glory, that we may see the most important results of this our cosmography in the fulfilment of the holy words of the Gospel.

On board the ship *Dolphin*, in the port of Dieppe in Normandy, the 8th of July, 1524.

Your humble servitor,

JANUS VERRAZZANUS.

A letter from President Jeannin to Henry IV. of France, written at The Hague, and dated January 1st, 1609, follows:

Sɪʀ :—Some time ago, I made, by your Majesty's order, overtures to an Amsterdam merchant, named Isaac Le Maire, a wealthy man of considerable experience in the East India trade.　He offered to make himself useful to your Majesty in matters of this kind, and intends to form (for this purpose) an association with some other merchants.　He also wishes to engage the services of some mariners, pilots, and sailors acquainted with northern navigation, whose services he has provisionally retained.　He has now repeatedly urged me to give him an answer, and I have always told him that your Majesty could not come to any decision in this affair before it had been settled whether the present negotiations to obtain a truce for the States General would be successful or not.　Le Maire considered this to be perfectly fair, and was satisfied with the answer.　But a few days ago he sent to me his brother to inform me that an English pilot, who has twice sailed in search of a northern passage, has been called to Amsterdam by the East India Company, to tell them what he had found and whether he hoped to discover that passage.　They had been well satisfied with his answer, and had thought they might succeed in the scheme.　They had, however, been unwilling to undertake at once the said expedition, and they had only remunerated the Englishman for his trouble, and had dismissed him with the promise of employing him next year, 1610.

The Englishman having thus obtained his leave, Le Maire, who knows him well, has since conferred

with him, and had learnt his opinions on these subjects; with regard to which the Englishman had also
held intercourse with Plancius, a great geographer and
clever mathematician. Plancius maintains, according
to the reasons of his science, and from other information given him, both by the Englishman and other
pilots, who have been engaged in the same navigation,
that there must be in the northern parts a passage corresponding to the one found near the south pole by
Magellan. One of these pilots has been there three
(thirteen) years ago, engaged in the same search, and
had gone as far as Nova Zembla, which is situated
under the seventy-third degree of latitude, on the coast
of the sea of Tartary towards the north. This pilot has
declared that he was at that time not sufficiently experienced, and that instead of penetrating into the open
sea, which is never frozen, on account of its depth and
of the great force of its currents and waves, he kept
near the coast. He there found the sea frozen, and
both he and his companions were prevented from penetrating any further, and were obliged to return.

The Englishman also reports that having been to
the north as far as eighty degrees, he has found that
the more northward he went the less cold it became;
and that whilst in Nova Zembla the land was barren
and there were none but carnivorous animals of prey,
like bears, foxes, and the like, he had found under the
eighty-first degree grass on the ground, and animals
that lived on it. Plancius confirms this by scientific
reasons, and says that near the pole the sun shines for

five months continually; and although his rays are weak, yet on account of the long time they continue, they have sufficient strength to warm the ground, to render it temperate, to accommodate it for the habitation of men, and to produce grass for the nourishment of animals. He compares it to a small fire, which is but lighted and then immediately extinguished. He also adds that one ought to be satisfied with the opinion of the ancients, who considered the regions around the poles as uninhabitable on account of their cold, and that they have been mistaken in this respect as much as they have been with regard to the tropics, which they also considered uninhabitable on account of their great heat. For the tropics have, nevertheless, been proved habitable, temperate, fertile, and favourable to the existence of man; and there is more heat on the borders of the tropics than near the line. For this reason Plancius thinks that the cold increases (as you proceed from the north pole), and that it is greatest under the seventieth degree; but that passing nearer to the pole it becomes less. Thus the Englishman and other pilots who have gone to these regions have found it to be; and they conclude that to find the northern passage with greater ease, we ought not to sail along the coasts in the 70, 71, 72, and 73 degrees, as the Dutch have done; but that, on the contrary, we ought to advance into the open sea, and so go as far as to the 81, 82, and 83 degrees, or even further if necessary; because the sea not being frozen in that latitude, they trust to be able to find the passage; and then sailing

eastwards, to pass through the Straits of Anian, and
then following the east coast of Tartary, so go to the
kingdom of Cathay, to China, to the Islands of Japan,
and also to the Spice Islands, and the Philippines. For
east and west join on account of the spherical shape of
our earth. This whole voyage, both out and home,
can be finished in six months, without approaching
any of the harbours and fortresses of the King of
Spain; whilst by the road round the Cape of Good
Hope, which is now in common use, one generally re-
quires three years, and one is besides exposed to meet
and fight the Portuguese.

He proposed to me in his overtures with regard to
the northern passage, that your Majesty might undertake the search openly and in your Majesty's name, as
a glorious enterprise, or else under the name of some
private man, whose success, if good, would not fail to
be attributed to the king. Le Maire offered, in the
name of his brother Isaac, to furnish the vessel and the
crew, unless your Majesty should wish to employ some
of her own men, together with those whom he would
send out and who are experienced in this kind of navigation. He says that to execute this enterprise he
would require but three or four thousand crowns at
the utmost, which money he wishes to obtain from
your Majesty because he, who is a private man, would
not lay out so large a sum; nor does he dare to speak
about it to any one because the East India Company
fears above everything to be forestalled in this design.
Therefore Isaac Le Maire would not converse about

this matter with the Englishman except in secret.   He
also adds that if this passage be discovered, it will
greatly facilitate the means of forming an association
to traffic with all these countries ; and that more people
will engage their capital in the new society than in the
East India Company, which is already in existence.
The East India Company will not even have a right to
complain, because the charter granted to them by the
States General authorises them to sail only round the
Cape of Good Hope, and not by the north.   Of this
latter passage the States have reserved to themselves
the right of granting the privilege in case it should be
discovered.   And in order to encourage some bold
pilots to undertake this search, they promised a reward
of 80,000 livres to the first discoverer.

I told the brother of Le Maire who had made me
these overtures, and I have also written to him, that I
would immediately submit the matter to your Majesty,
to know your pleasure, and that I would inform him
of it as soon as possible ; for he says that if one wishes
to engage in this voyage in the present year, one must
begin it in March at the very latest, if any success is to
be hoped from it.   Others who have before begun it in
July have suffered greatly and have been overtaken by
the winter.   Having also been informed that Plancius
had come to The Hague two days after the above conversation, I invited him to call upon me, in order to
speak with him.   This I have done, without however
letting him know that Le Maire had made overtures to
me, for Le Maire wishes nobody to be aware of it.

Therefore I have spoken to Plancius only in the way of a scientific discussion on the northern passage, and as if I were desirous to instruct myself, and to learn what he knows about it or what he concludes, on scientific grounds. He has confirmed to me all the above facts, and he also told me that it was he who incited the late Jacob Heemskirk, the admiral of the fleet which beat the Spaniards in the Straits of Gibraltar, to undertake the above enterprise. Heemskirk had consented to do so, and Plancius had expected great achievements from him, because Heemskirk was greatly experienced in navigation and was anxious to acquire the honour of finding a passage through the Arctic Regions, like Magellan, who had discovered the passage to the South Sea. But Heemskirk fell in that battle in the Straits of Gibraltar.

It belongs to your Majesty to command me what I am to do in this affair. The truth is that one cannot guarantee the success of this enterprise with certainty; but yet it is also true that Le Maire has for a long time inquired into the chances of the undertaking, and that he is generally considered to be an able and industrious man. Besides, the risk would not be very great When Ferdinand of Spain received the offer of Columbus, and caused three ships to be fitted out for him to sail to the West Indies, the proposal seemed still more hazardous, and all the other potentates to whom he had applied had laughed at him, considering his success as impossible, and yet he has obtained such great results. It is also the opinion of Plancius, and of other geographers, that in the northern parts there are many countries which have not yet been discovered, and which God may be keeping for the glory and profit of other princes, unwilling to give everything to Spain alone. Even were nothing to come of this search, yet it would always be honourable to have undertaken it, and the regret will not be very great since so little is risked.

This letter having been terminated, and I being ready to send it to your Majesty, Le Maire has again written to me, and has sent to me the memoir, which is joined to the present letter, which also contains an ample discussion of the above subject. He also writes to me that some members of the East India Company, who had been informed that the Englishman had secretly treated with him, had become afraid that I might wish to employ him for the discovery of this passage. For this reason, they have again treated with him about his undertaking such an expedition in the course of the present year. The directors of the Amsterdam chamber have written to the other chambers of the same company to request their approval; and should the others refuse, the Amsterdam chamber will undertake the expedition at their own risk. Le Maire, nevertheless, persists in advising your Majesty to engage in this enterprise, telling me that he has at his disposal a pilot who has already been engaged in a similar voyage, and who is more experienced and more capable than the Englishman.

It belongs to your Majesty to order what I am to do.

I have had several conferences with other men about expeditions to the West and East Indies, and I feel confident that when it will please your Majesty to take the matter into serious consideration, with the intention of profiting by it, there will be means of obtaining very able and experienced men. There are also many rich merchants who will gladly join in the commerce with East India, and yet more willingly if this northern passage be found; but as to the West Indies, they all think that far greater armaments will be required. It is true that the voyage is also shorter, and those who have some knowledge of the intercourse which may be established with those parts, promise great success. They also prove this by such good reasons that we may well believe them. I am expecting your Majesty's commands, praying God, sire, that he may give to your Majesty and to the whole Royal family all happiness and prosperity.

P. JEANNIN.

The Hague, the 25th of January, 1609.

EXTRACT FROM JOHN DE LAET'S "NEW WORLD," RELATING TO HUDSON'S THIRD VOYAGE

As to the first discovery, the directors of the privileged East India Company in 1609 dispatched the yacht *Half Moon* under the command of Henry Hudson, captain and supercargo, to seek a passage to China by the north-east; but he changed his course and stood over towards New France, and having passed the banks of

Newfoundland in latitude forty-three degrees twenty-three minutes, he made the land in latitude forty-four degrees fifteen minutes, with a west north-west and north-west course, and went on shore at a place where there were many of the natives, with whom, as he understood, the French came every year to trade. Sailing thence he bent his course to the south, until running south south-west and south-west by south he again made land in latitude forty-one degrees forty-three minutes, which he supposed to be an island and gave it the name of New Holland, but afterwards discovered that it was Cape Cod, and that according to his observation to lay two hundred and twenty-five miles to the west of its place on all the charts. Pursuing his course to the south he again saw land in latitude thirty-seven degrees fifteen minutes. The coast was low, running north and south, and opposite to it lay a bank or shoal within which there was a depth of eight, nine, ten, eleven, seven, and six and one-half fathoms, with a sandy bottom. Hudson called this place Dry Cape. (This was probably Cape Charles near the mouth of the Chesapeake Bay.)

Changing his course to the northward he again discovered land in latitude thirty-eight degrees nine minutes, where there was a white sandy shore, and within appeared a thick grove of trees full of green foliage. The direction of the coast was north north-east and south south-west for about twenty-four miles, then north and south for twenty-one miles, and afterwards south-east and north-west for fifteen miles. They con-

tinued to run along this coast to the north until they
reached a point from which the land stretched to the
west and north-west, where several rivers discharged
into an open bay. Land was seen to the east north-
east, which Hudson first took to be an island, but
proved to be the main land, and the second point of
the bay, in latitude thirty-eight degrees fifty-four minutes. Standing in upon a course north-west by west
they soon found themselves embayed, and encountering
many breakers stood out again to the south south-east.
Hudson suspected that a large river discharged into
the bay from the current which set out and because of
the accumulation of sands and shoals. Continuing
their course along the shore to the north they observed a white sandy beach, and drowned land within,
beyond which there appeared a grove of wood, the
coast running north-east by east and south-west by
south. Afterwards the direction of the coast changed
to north by east and was higher land than they had
yet seen. They at length reached a lofty promontory
or head-land, behind which was situated a bay, which
they entered and ran up into a roadstead near a low
sandy point, in latitude forty degrees and eighteen
minutes. There they were visited by two savages
clothed in elk skins, and who showed them every sign
of friendship. On the land they found an abundance
of blue plums and magnificent oaks of a height and
thickness one seldom sees, together with poplars and
linden trees and various other kinds of wood useful
in ship building. Sailing hence in a north-easterly

direction they ascended the river to nearly forty-three degrees north latitude, where it became so narrow and of so little depth that they found it necessary to return.

From what they could learn there had never been any ships nor christians in that quarter before and they were the first to discover the river and ascend it so far. Henry Hudson returned to Amsterdam with this report and in the following year, 1610, some merchants again sent a ship thither, that is to say, to the second river discovered, which was called Manhattes, from the savage nation that dwelt at its mouth, and subsequently their High Mightinesses the States-General granted to these merchants the exclusive privilege of navigating this river and trading there. Whereupon in the year 1615 a redoubt or fort was erected on the river and occupied by a small garrison of which we shall speak here-after. Our countrymen have continued to make voyages thither from year to year, to the purpose of trafficking with the natives, and on this account the country has very justly received the name New Netherland.

VAN METEREN'S ACCOUNT OF HUDSON'S THIRD VOYAGE.

In estimating the value of Van Meteren's story we must take into consideration the acquaintance that probably existed between the historian and the navigator. Dr. Asher is of the opinion that the correspondence between Hudson and the Dutch East India Company passed through the hands of Van

Meteren, who was at the time Dutch Consul in London. Nothing would be more natural than to suppose that Van Meteren received from Hudson a personal account of his adventures. To Van Meteren's story we owe our knowledge of the mutiny of the crew of the *Half Moon* in 1609; a subject upon which Juet preserved a discreet silence.

The following quotation is from Van Meteren's *Historie Der Nederlanden*, the translation here furnished being that made by Dr. Asher, and published by the Hakluyt Society along with the original Dutch text, in 1860.

We have observed in our last book, that the directors of the Dutch East India Company sent out in March last year, on purpose to seek a passage to China by North-east or North-west, an experienced English pilot named Henry Hudson (te weten een Kloeck Enghels Piloot Herry Hutson, ghenoemt), in a vlie boat, having a crew of eighteen or twenty hands, partly English, partly Dutch. This Henry Hudson left the Texel the 6th of April (new style), 1609, and having doubled the cape of Norway the 5th of May, directed his course along the northern coast towards Nova Zembla; but he there found the sea as full of ice as he had found it the preceding year, so that he lost the hope of effecting anything during the season. This circumstance, and the cold which some of his men who had been in the East Indies could not bear, caused quarrels among the crew, they being partly English, partly Dutch; upon which the captain, Henry Hudson, laid before them two propositions; the first of these was, to go to the coast of America to the latitude of 408. This idea had been suggested to him by some letters and maps which his friend, Captain Smith, had sent him from Virginia, and by which he informed him that there was a sea leading to the Western ocean, by the north of the Southern English Colony. Had this information been true (experience goes as yet to the contrary), it would have been of great advantage, as indicating a short way to India. The other proposition was, to direct their search to Davis Straits. This meeting with general approval, they sailed on the 14th of May, and arrived with a good wind at the Faroe Islands, where they stopped but twenty-four hours to supply themselves with fresh water. After leaving these islands, they sailed on till, on the 18th of July, they reached the coast of Nova Francia, under 44°, where they were obliged to land for the purpose of getting a new foremast, having lost theirs. They found this a good place for cod fishing, as also for traffic in skins and furs, which were to be got there at a very low price. But the crew behaved badly towards the people of the country, taking their property by force, out of which arose quarrels among them. The English fearing that they would be out-numbered and worsted, were therefore afraid to make any further attempt. They left that place on the 26th of July, and kept out at sea till the 3d of August, when they were again near the coast in 42° of latitude.

Thence they sailed on till on the 12th of August we (*sic*) reached 40° 45′, where they found a good entrance, between two headlands, and thus entered on the 12th of September, into as fine a river as can be found, with fine anchoring ground on both sides.

Their ship sailed up the river as far as 42° 40′. Then their boat went higher up. Along the river they found sensible and warlike people; whilst in the highest part the people were more friendly and had an abundance of provisions, skins and furs of martins and foxes, and many other commodities, as birds and fruit; even white and red grapes. These Indians traded most amicably with people from the ship; and of all the above mentioned commodities they brought some home. When they had thus been about fifty leagues up the river they returned on the 4th of October and went again to sea. More could have been done if the crew had been willing and the want of some necessary provisions had not prevented it. While at sea they held council together, but were of different opinions. The mate, a Dutchman, advised to winter in Newfoundland (de onder Schipper een Nederlander, was Van Meyninghe op Jerra Nova, te gaen verwinterin), and to search the Northwestern passage of Davis throughout. This was opposed by Hudson. *He was afraid of his mutinous crew, who had sometimes savagely threatened him*, and he feared that during the cold season they would entirely consume their provisions and would then be obliged to return.

Many of the crew also were ill and sickly. Nobody, however, spoke of returning to Holland, which circumstance made the captain still more suspicious. He proposed, therefore, to sail to Ireland, and winter there ; which they all agreed to. At last they arrived at Dartmouth, in England, the 7th of November, whence they informed their employers, the directors of the East India Company, of their voyage.

BY PETER STUYVESANT.—A REPORT TO THE WEST INDIA COMPANY.

From a translation published in Brodhead's Documents relating to the History of New York. Vol. II, page 412.

Touching the second subject of your letter (that his Majesty hath commanded you, in his name, to require a surrender of all such forts, towns, or places of strength, which now are possessed by the Dutch within my government), I answer : That we give his Majesty of Great Britain credit for so much discretion and equity, in case his Majesty were informed and instructed correctly and truly that the Dutch came into these Provinces not of their own authority, but by virtue of commission granted to private individuals by their High Mightinesses, the Lord's States-General of the United Netherlands, had settled themselves in this Province first of all in the years 1614, 1615 and 1616, upon this North river, near Fort Orange, where, to hinder the invasions and massacres of the savages, they had built a little fort ; and after, in the year 1622 and following years even to this present time, by virtue of commission and grant from the Lord's States-General to the directors of the Incorporated West India Company, and, moreover, in the year 1656, of a grant of the South river to the Honorable, the Burgomasters or Amsterdam, insomuch, that, by virtue of the abovesaid commissions from the High and Mighty States-General, given to the above mentioned and other private persons, this Province has been possessed and governed; when (we say) his Majesty is correctly informed of all this and what more might be said in regard of the first discovery, uninterrupted possession, prior purchase of the lands of the Native Princes and owners of the country (though heathens) we are fully persuaded that his Majesty's justice would not in a time when so close a friendship and union have been so recently made, grant such an order to disturb their High Mightinesses' subjects in this New Netherland Province, much less to demand its surrender and that of the places and fortresses which their High Mightinesses, the Lords States-General, order and direct us to maintain, preserve and protect in their name, by their commission dated 28th July, 1646, as the same was exhibited to your Deputies on the day before yesterday, 20th/30th ult., under their High Mightinesses' hands and seal.

Among the valuable documents preserved through the joint instrumentality of several people, there is an account of the Greenland or Grönland colonies, written by a native of the North during the sixteenth century. This narrative or treatise, by Ivar Bardsen or Boty, is regarded by historians as being of authentic value. It was translated into several languages and a copy finally fell into the hands of Henry Hudson. The copy which he had came into the possession of Richard Hakluyt and subsequently was owned by the Rev. Samuel Purchas. It was prefaced by a note in Hudson's own handwriting.

"A treatise of Ivar Boty, a Gronlander, translated out of the Norsh Language into High Dutch in the year 1560, and afterwards out of High Dutch into Low Dutch by William Barentsen of Amsterdam, who was chief pilot aforesaid. The same copy in High Dutch is in the hands of Iodicus Hondius, which I have seen. This was translated out of Low Dutch by Master William Stere, merchant in the year 1608, for the use of me, Henry Hudson. William Barentsen's book is in the hands of Master Peter Plantius, who lent the same to me."

It is evident from the foregoing that Hudson received this treatise from William Stere after his first voyage to the Greenland coast and before his celebrated third voyage. Its possession may well have influenced his action when upon the third voyage he was forced to abandon his projected course to the north-east.

Apart from its significance as a possible factor in the great voyage, the treatise of Boty has a greatly augmented value from the fact that the preface just quoted must set at rest several questions regarding Hudson's relations with the navigators and geographers of his day, his retention of the English spelling of his name, and his inability to read Dutch with ease, if at all.

A letter or remonstrance addressed to the Lords States-General of Holland from the Assembly of XIX. The original preserved in the Royal Archives at The Hague:

HIGH AND MIGHTY LORDS:

The deputies of the Assembly of the XIX. are instructed to complain to your High Mightinesses that one Jacob Jacobsen Elkins, having entered the service of Mr. William Klobery and his assistants, with the ship *The William*, whereof William Trevor was Master, did in the year 1633 in the month of April come to the North River in New Netherland . . . in order to exchange his merchandise . . . under feigned pretense that the said river and adjacent country were in and of the domain of his Majesty of Great Britain . . . without however being willing to exhibit, when demanded by our agents, his Majesty's instruction or commission. . . . Nevertheless it is sufficiently notorious to all the world, and he, Jacob Elkins himself knows best of all (having been employed even before the year 1614 in the service of those who then had your High Mightinesses grant to trade, exclusively, to the river and surrounding places) that said river and adjacent country had been discovered in the year 1609 at the cost of the East India Company, before any Christian had ever been up said river, *as Hudson testified, who was then in the service of the said Company, for the purpose of discovering the North-west passage to China.*

An extract from memoir of English encroachments upon New Netherland, drawn up from various documents in the archives of the West India Company in January, 1656:

In the year 1610 some merchants again (following Hudson's voyage) sent a ship thither from this country and obtained afterwards from the High and Mighty Lords States-General a grant to resort and trade exclusively to those parts, to which end they likewise in the year 1615 built on the North River about the Manhattans, a redoubt or little fort, where was left a small garrison, some people usually remaining to carry on trade with the natives or Indians. This was continued and maintained until their High Mightinesses did in the year 1622 include this country of New Netherland in the charter of the West India Company.

INDEX

A

Adrey, John, 70
Aerssens, Francis, 103
Africa, 247
Albany, 152, 160, 163, 220–222
Algonquin or Algonkin Lenape Indians, 157
Alva, Ferdinand Alvarez de Toledo, Duke of A., 89, 216
Amsterdam, vii., 20, 26, 27, 38, 66, 90, 93, 97–101, 108, 112, 114, 206, 215, 221, 250, 260
Amsterdam Chamber (of E. I. Co.), 256
Amundsen, Capt. Roald, 205
Angelo, Michael, v.
Antartic, the, 53
Antwerp, 38, 89
Archangel, port of, 12, 13
Arctic Ocean, the, 99
Arena Islands, 174
Aristotle, 247
Ark Raleigh, The, 33
Arnall, or Arnold, Ladlie, Lodlo, or Ladlow, 70, 74, 186, 199, 200, 203
Asher, Dr. Georg M., 14, 64, 66, 76, 79, 112, 127, 147, 154, 206, 260, 261
Asia, 246, 247
Atlantis, 82
Aubert, Master Thomas, 22
Austria, 86

B

Baffin, William, 205
Bahamas, the, 64
Baltic, the, 16

Bantam, 187
Barents, Barentz, Barentsen, or Barentzoon, William, 26, 39, 56, 57, 66, 67, 93, 96, 266
Barnes, John, 70
Barneveld, John of (Olden), 86, 90, 91, 102, 104, 175
Barton, Dr., 140
Bayonne, 148
Bay Ridge, 148
Baxter, Thomas, 46
Beekman, Col. William, 224
Beeren Island, 26
Bellamont, Earl of, 223, 225
Bergen, 16, 148
Beuberry, James, 45
Beveren, Sieur de, 8, 21, 22
Bikker, Gerret, 27
Billet, or Bylot, Robert, 179, 187, 190, 192, 194, 199, 204
Bishop's Gate, London, 44, 45
Blackwall, 69, 179
Boty, 39 ; or Barsden, Ivar, 266
Braunch, John, 70
Bridewell, 69
British East India Co., 15
Broadhead, John Romeyn, viii., 94, 127, 264
Broket, 112
Bruges, 6, 89
Brunswick, 17
Brussels, 97
Burghers of Free Town, 17
Burough, Stephen, 79
Buss Island, 114
Bute, Michael, 199, 200, 203

C

Cabot, Sebastian, 2. 8, 21, 28, 39, 44, 79, 96, 151

ABOUT THE AUTHOR

Edgar Mayhew Bacon was born a U.S. citizen in Nassau in 1855 and spent most of his life in the Tarrytown, New York area. Before becoming a historian and writer, he worked in a bookstore in Albany. He married Anna Beard in 1903. He was a member of the Reformed Dutch Church of Tarrytown, American Historians Association, and the National Geographic Society. He also wrote *Chronicles of Tarrytown and Sleepy Hollow*. He died in 1935 and is buried at the Sleepy Hollow Cemetery in New York.

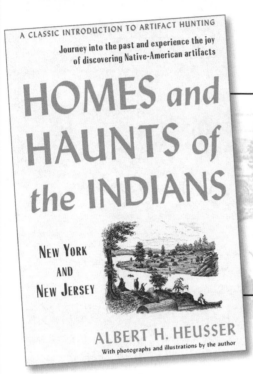

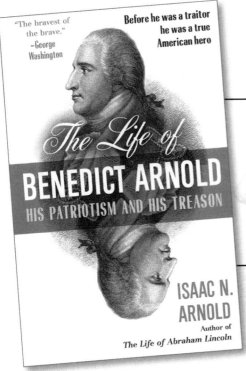